D1622446

A BETTER START
NEW CHOICES
FOR EARLY LEARNING

A BETTER START
NEW CHOICES FOR
EARLY LEARNING

EDITED BY
FRED M. HECHINGER

WALKER AND COMPANY, NEW YORK

First published in the United States of America in 1986 by the Walker Publishing Company, Inc.

Published simultaneously in Canada by John Wiley & Sons Canada, Limited, Rexdale, Ontario.

Library of Congress Cataloging-in-Publication Data

A better start.

   Bibliography: p.
   Includes index.
   1. Education, Preschool—United States. 2. Day care centers—United States. 3. Domestic education—United States. I. Hechinger, Fred M.
LB1140.23.B48   1986   372'.21   86-15711
ISBN 0-8027-0897-8

ISBN: 0-8027-0897-8

ISBN: 0-8027-7300-1 {paper}

Printed in the United States of America

10 9 8 7 6 5 4 3 2 1

Book design by Joan Willens

For Grace

CONTENTS

CONTRIBUTORS

W. Steven Barnett, formerly an economist with the High/Scope Educational Research Foundation, is now a research associate with the Early Intervention Research Institute at Utah State University.

John R. Berrueta-Clement, formerly a research coordinator at the High/Scope Educational Research Foundation, is now with the Governmental Activities Office of the American Federation of Information Processing Societies.

Marilyn R. Bradbard is an associate professor in the Department of Family and Child Development at Auburn University.

Nancy Curry is a professor in the School of Health-Related Professions at the University of Pittsburgh and director of its Program in Child Development and Child Care.

Richard C. Endsley is a professor in the Department of Child and Family Development at the University of Georgia.

Ann S. Epstein is a Senior Research Associate with the High/Scope Educational Research Foundation.

Donald H. Graves is a professor of education at the University of New Hampshire and Director of the Atkinson Writing Project.

Fred M. Hechinger is president of *The New York Times* Company Foundation and education columnist for the *Times*. He was that newspaper's education editor for ten years and later a member of its editorial board. In 1966, he edited *Pre-School Education Today*. Among his other books is *Growing Up in America,* co-authored with his wife Grace.

Mary B. Larner is a research associate at the High/Scope Educational Research Foundation.

Donald E. Pierson is director of the Brookline Early Education Project, Brookline, Massachusetts.

Tony Schwartz is a journalist, currently a contributing editor to *New York Magazine,* and formerly a reporter for *The New York Times.*

Lawrence J. Schweinhart is director of the Voices for Children Project at the High/Scope Educational Research Foundation.

Virginia Stuart teaches writing at the University of New Hampshire. She is coauthor of *Resources for Gifted Children.*

Terrence Tivnan is an assistant professor in the Harvard Graduate School of Education.

Deborah Klein Walker is an assistant professor at the Harvard Schools of Public Health and Education.

David P. Weikart is president of the High/Scope Educational Research Foundation. He is principal investigator for the Perry Preschool Study.

Mildred M. Winter, a consultant in early childhood education for the Missouri Department of Elementary and Secondary Education, is state project director of the Parents as First Teachers program.

Edward Zigler is Sterling Professor of Psychology at Yale University and director of the Bush Center in Child Development and Social Policy. He is a former director of the Office of Child Development and chief of the Children's Bureau at HEW.

A BETTER START
NEW CHOICES
FOR EARLY LEARNING

CHAPTER ONE

INTRODUCTION: A Better Start

Fred M. Hechinger

Most of our children deserve a better start.

The fairy tale vision of childhood in America sees happy toddlers playing in the backyard under mother's watchful eyes. While keeping the house spotless, mother also manages to play with her youngsters, read stories to them, prepare lunch and an afternoon snack with visiting neighborhood children possibly on hand, and have dinner on the table when hubby comes home from work. In an urban setting, mother finds time, twice a day, to take the children to the park. In rich households, mother delegates some of those functions to a highly trained nanny. By the time these youngsters enter kindergarten or first grade, they have already learned to read and to count. They have played with educational toys. They are ready for academic success.

Most Americans know this idyllic description for what it is—a nostalgic backward glance to a world long past. Only uninformed politicians still pretend this ideal vision represents the way American children today live during the crucial first five years of their lives. Only self-deceiving moralizers continue to admonish women to do their motherly task by tending only to their kitchens and their children.

The advantage of these illusions is that they justify inaction, and that saves money. Mother's work, after all, does not cost anything.

The reality, of course, is quite different. Mother, in increasing numbers of families, is not at home during much of the day; she is out and at work. In 1984, 48 percent of women with infants under one year old were in the labor force, and there

1

were over twenty million children under 13 years of age with working mothers, including nine million under age six. It therefore is no longer a question whether it is better for children in their early years to be tended by their mothers; it is simply a fact that about half of all mothers with small children work. In the years ahead, that number will grow. Modern economics make this inevitable, not only for single mothers but for old-fashioned families as well.

These simple facts illustrate the need for new arrangements to care for children in their early years. This includes simple child care and what has come to be known as early childhood education.

What has put the spotlight on those new needs is the plight of poor children. Their neglect has long been sending them to school with serious deficits in cognitive skills and in social behavior. They have grown up in a generally nonverbal and often illiterate environment. Their homes are devoid of books, of art, of adults who speak to them, encourage them to ask questions, and answer when questions are asked. While those deficits are most devastating for children of the poor, they are of increasing concern also for children of affluent families. Frequently, the television set becomes the babysitter, leaving youngsters inactive and exposed to an unmonitored impact of a medium that, with rare exceptions, presents intellectual fare that is unsuitable for children, and often downright harmful.

The labor market does not provide an adequate supply of literate substitutes for mothers: children are often left to the care of only marginally literate women who may speak little English. In many day-care centers, similarly inadequate persons are hired. This amounts at best to safe storage; it is hardly an adequate substitute for old-fashioned home care.

Project Head Start, created in 1965, was the first organized and largely government-financed answer to the intellectual and social neglect of poor children before they entered school or kindergarten. The preschool education concept had come late to the United States. Almost all other industrial societies in which both parents need to be away from home have devised and financed some form of preschool care and education. In Scandinavia, for instance, most corporations provide daytime child care centers. (In the United States, even today, only 1,850 of the nation's six million employers provide any form of such day care, either directly or indirectly.)

By 1965, it had become evident that many poor children needed a head start to be able to compete in school on anything approaching an equal basis with their more fortunate contemporaries. Benjamin S. Bloom, in his experimental work and in his book, *Stability and Change in Human Characteristics*, had shown that the long-term effect of living in a culturally deprived environment was likely to lower a child's measured intelligence by up to twenty IQ points, an enormous difference in terms of the capacity to learn and of society's and the school's expectations. Such a deficit could make the difference between a youngster thought to be barely educable for unskilled labor and one who could succeed in college. The point made by Dr. Bloom and others, including Dr. Bruno Bettelheim, the noted child psychiatrist, was that a sensible change in environment could transform children's potential. Head Start, as an organized approach to preschool education, promised such a transformation.

For largely political and fiscal reasons, the debate over the effect of Head Start continues two decades later. Its critics point out that the gains shown by Head Start youngsters when they entered school often were wiped out by the time they entered third or fourth grade; but it is fair to suggest that this may be the schools' inability to offer the same kind of special care and attention that children received in at least the high-quality preschool education programs. A sensible response might have been to make preschool education even more effective and to make the subsequent follow-through more intensive as well. One frequently overlooked need is to provide elementary school teachers with a better understanding of the teaching skills and qualities that worked in the preschool approach.

On the whole, however, the impact of Head Start, as a first step toward effective preschool education and child care, was sufficiently favorable to lead to demands for the next step: early childhood education. This time, the proponents of such a radical departure from the traditional start of education, somewhere between the ages of five and six, provided convincing evidence to the profession, the public and the politicians who ultimately control the pursestrings. The longitudinal study by the High/Scope Educational Research Foundation for more than 16 years followed children who had benefited from high-quality early childhood education, and those who had not. The results, as told in the report, "Changed Lives," excerpts from which follow, showed that black youngsters from the depths of poverty, who had been enrolled at age 3 in high-quality early childhood education programs, were far less likely to fail in school, to get into conflict with the law, to become unemployed and, in the case of the girls, to become pregnant as teenagers.

The High/Scope experiment, carried out in the Perry Elementary School of Ypsilanti, Michigan, and supported by the Carnegie Corporation of New York, dealt with poor black children in dire need of special attention; but the advantages such early education offered to them must be considered applicable as well to children of affluent working parents. The time has come for a careful look at early childhood education as the next step toward fuller educational and developmental opportunities for American children.

A hard look at some basic facts ought to justify major, initially costly, changes in the nation's approach to the development and education of very young children. Contrary to the widespread belief that the poor constitute only a small minority, the fact is that in 1985 of all children under age six, one in four lived in poverty. In seventeen states more than one fourth of preschool children are in homes below the poverty line. The High/Scope Educational Research Foundation warns that "without more help than they now get, these impoverished children are likely to grow up without the chance, as adults, to make productive contributions to society;" instead, they will be costly, and potentially dangerous, liabilities for the rest of their lives.

Currently, 29 percent of the nation's poor three- and four-year-olds are enrolled in preschool programs that provide some, though not necessarily adequate, educational activities. The Federal government spends about one billion dollars a year on Head Start and another billion on care for low-income children. About a dozen states add their own money, estimated at a total of $225 million.

Between 1970 and 1983, the enrollment rate of three- and four-year-olds from poor and affluent families in some kind of program has risen from 21 to 38 percent. Mothers who work outside the home make a variety of arrangements: seven out of ten children are cared for in their own homes or in the homes of others. Two out of five children are cared for by relatives. Nearly one out of ten accompanies the mother to work, and 15 percent are in day-care centers.

Head Start's original purpose—helping disadvantaged children to move into the mainstream—has created the impression that early childhood education and day care are for the poor only; in fact, affluent parents are far more likely to send their children to organized preschool education programs at age three or even younger. For families with incomes below $20,000, the preschool enrollment rate is 46 percent; for families with higher incomes, it is 64 percent. The selection of better programs by those who can afford to pay for them makes the gap between rich and poor infinitely wider.

Even though usually not compulsory, kindergarten has become nearly universal, and there are many good ones. Finding good day care and preschools is far more difficult, and not only for the poor. Running a good program is costly and calls for a great deal of professional skill in management and staff. In an article in *The New York Times,* Tony Schwartz, a writer and editor, reported that the center his daughter has attended ever since she was 6 months old is always under a money crunch. "The simple truth," wrote Mr. Schwartz, "is that it is extremely difficult to operate a self-supporting high quality facility without charging rates so high that most families cannot possibily afford them. And while there is some public support for parents at the lowest end of the income scale, there's not nearly enough to make quality care available to all working parents."

Yet, strong and vocal opposition to institutional services for young children persists despite all the evidence of the benefits. The persuasive findings of the High/Scope experiment no longer stand alone. Other experiments, independently carried out, have corroberated the findings. For example, Martin Deutsch and Cynthia P. Deutsch, of New York University, among the country's leading researchers of early child development, have carried out their own long-term studies and arrived at virtually the same conclusions as High/Scope. Moreover, they have responded to the objection that early gains among disadvantaged children tend to be wiped out soon after the youngsters enter elementary school. They call this "washout of initial gains" entirely understandable: after all, they say, if youngsters have responded to a system of special support and encouragement, is it not natural for them to regress when special supports and encouragements are withdrawn and they are thrown back into an indifferent environment?

Not unlike Ypsilanti, the Deutsches created an early childhood education program in the Institute for Developmental Studies which dealt with children from New York City's Harlem community. By the time they were between nineteen and twenty-one years old, those who had participated in the IDS program showed the following advantages over those who had not (their comparative figures are given in parentheses): employed, 49 percent (24); graduated from high school, 58 percent (40); attend college or vocational training, 39 percent (28). Not unlike the Michigan approach, the Harlem experiment stressed intellectual stimulation, questioning, verbal communications and a variety of technological teaching aids. With financing from the Ford Foundation, the program included a mandatory breakfast. Books were provided to create a parent-child reading program. Each preschool class of seventeen children had one teacher and a specially trained teacher's aide.

Early childhood education and care clearly are not confined to the poor. For instance, the State of Vermont has issued a "Handbook for Improving Early Education" by James G. Lengel of the state's Department of Education. Its chapter on Developmental Care for Three and Four Year Olds provides guidelines which largely parallel the Michigan experiment.

Beyond a doubt, early childhood education is the next step

in efforts to deal with the majority of the nation's children and to come to grips with the terrifying build-up of social and intellectual deficits among children of poverty. If the early 1960's ushered in significant experiments in early childhood education and child care, it was in 1985 that the fruits of those experiments were finally being reaped. A recent survey by *Education Week* showed that at least 28 states have initiated early childhood education programs.

With so much activity in an area that is still new and unconventional, some opposition, or at least concerned questioning, are to be expected. Money is clearly an issue, particularly at a time when all existing education programs are threatened with budget cuts. But beyond dollars, legitimate questions are being raised by some experts about the effect of early childhood education on children. Will these formal programs for the very young, even infants, aggravate middle-class parental tendencies to subject their children to inappropriate academic drill? Will parental anxieties about their children's chances of getting into high-prestige colleges be translated into premature reading and writing instruction? Will formal schooling come too soon, depriving youngsters of a normal carefree childhood?

These questions should indeed be asked at a time when early childhood education and day care are taking shape as mass enterprises. So the question should be whether the new enterprise, in full or in part, ought to become part of the public school system whose rigidities have often been accused of standing in the way particularly of poor children's learning.

Such questions can be debated, and eventually answered, without any retreat from the basic concept of early childhood education. The key to an answer is that the search is not simply for an earlier, but for a better start. At stake is a new and better deal for children, but always appropriate to their age, capacity and stage of growth. This means that childish play in a cosy, child-centered setting, under the guidance of warm and caring adults, is the absolute prerequisite. Early childhood education must not be a case of "too much too soon" but of providing the right and timely kind of nurture of mind and body.

The experience of a literate environment in a program for 3-year-olds may be a pleasant icing on a happy middle-class childhood; but for millions of poor children, many of whom would otherwise be doomed to lifelong failure, a better start can be a social, economic, and intellectual lifesaver. For them, an early opportunity to take part in a verbal, literate, caring way of life, for at least part of the day, is no frill; it could be the crucial chance to introduce them into the mainstream of American life. It offers no certainty, but at least opens the escape hatch from a growing underclass that threatens the future, not only of the economy but of a free society. As all responsible pioneers of early childhood education readily acknowledge, no educational strategy alone is a miracle cure for the nation's ills—not even for the problems of American education. Early childhood education will not wipe out unemployment or crime; but if it can cut either of those epidemic diseases by half, or even by 30 percent, the economic gain and the improvement of life in America would be worth the cost many times over. High/Scope estimates that every dollar spent on high-quality early childhood education will be repaid seven times over by the time the youngsters reach young adulthood. In terms of these children's chance to join in the pursuit of happiness, such gains exceed any dollar estimate.

As for questions raised about the inability of previous programs, such as Head Start, to close the gap between disadvantaged and affluent children, the answer is that wrong yardsticks are being used. Closing that gap must, of course, remain the ultimate goal; but for the moment, a more realistic and pertinent answer is that the programs have helped disadvantaged youngsters to do better when compared to others who have not been given the same opportunity.

The intent of this book is to bring together some of the pertinent facts about those new and promising ways of dealing with the minds, psyches, and bodies of young children to give them what all caring adults wish for each new generation: a better start. This slim volume does not claim to be complete in dealing with a field that remains in rapid growth and in flux. In selecting successful examples, I had to omit other equally promising programs.

I merely attempted to offer an insight into important and apparently successful research and development, first, to inform the lay reader about a vital trend. Such an initiation should serve parents and teachers with either a personal or a professional interest in giving youngsters a better start. For those who, for whatever reasons, wish to delve more deeply into this incipient revolution, the book paves the way for further reading and inquiry.

A second purpose, for lay and expert readers alike, is to provide a rough guide to the meaning of high-quality early childhood programs. No attempt is made to suggest definitive standards. It would be a dangerous folly to pretend that this is either possible or desirable. The only rough yardstick of quality is the extent to which children are made comfortable while their minds are opened and their imagination is engaged.

A third group of selections aims specifically at parents— how they can best take advantage of the new approaches; understanding what makes a good program and how to select the right one for their children. Parents are given a look at how they can help their children at home, specifically with the crucial skills of reading and writing.

Finally, a forum is given to respected experts and reporters who issue intelligent warnings against an overenthusiasm that could do harm to even the most promising new efforts. It would be irresponsible, for example, to ignore the cautionary views of Edward Zigler, one of Head Start's originators.

These caveats have been included, not to raise doubts about the crucial role early childhood education can play but rather to help avoid unnecessary pitfalls. Whatever the risks in moving ahead, the risks of standing still are infinitely greater. It is not enough to pay lip service to children as the nation's most precious resource; precious resources are readily squandered by lack of investment in them. Opportunities to break with failed habits do not come often. Can there be any doubt about past failures in dealing wisely with children? The nation cannot afford the cost of continued neglect; the price of lost human potential is incalculable; the time is now to offer all our children a better start.

CHAPTER TWO

CHANGED LIVES:
The Effects of the Perry Preschool Program on Youths Through Age 19

*by John R. Berrueta-Clement,
Lawrence J. Schweinhart, W. Steven
Barnett, Ann S. Epstein, and
David P. Weikart*

The Perry Preschool Project is a study of 123 black youths, from families of low socioeconomic status, who were at risk of failing in school. The purpose of the study, which began in 1962, is to explore the long-term effects on these young people of participation versus nonparticipation in a program of high quality early childhood education. Drawn from a single school attendance area, at ages three and four these youngsters were randomly divided into an experimental group that received a high quality preschool program and a control group that received no preschool program. Information about these youngsters on hundreds of variables has been collected and examined annually from ages three to eleven, and again at

---

This account of the landmark Perry Preschool study, supported by the Carnegie Corporation of New York, provides compelling evidence of early education's beneficial effects in school, employment, and society. This chapter comes from the monograph Changed Lives, *published by the High/Scope Educational Research Foundation, Ypsilanti, Michigan, in 1984.*

ages fourteen, fifteen, and nineteen—assessing family demographics; child abilities, attitudes, and scholastic accomplishments; and involvement in delinquent and criminal behavior, use of welfare assistance, and employment.

Results to age nineteen indicate lasting beneficial effects of preschool education in improving cognitive performance during early childhood; in improving scholastic placement and achievement during the school years; in decreasing delinquency and crime, the use of welfare assistance, and the incidence of teenage pregnancy; and in increasing high-school graduation rates and the frequency of enrollment in postsecondary programs and employment. The age nineteen findings are summarized in Table 1.

Preschool attendance altered performance by nearly a factor of two on four major variables at age nineteen. The rates of employment and participation in college or vocational training were nearly double for those with preschool as compared with those without preschool. For those who attended preschool, the rate of teenage pregnancy (including live births) and the percent of years spent in special education classes were

Table 1 MAJOR FINDINGS AT AGE 19
IN THE PERRY PRESCHOOL STUDY

Category	Number[a] Responding	Preschool Group	No-Preschool Group
Employed	121	59%	32%
High school graduation (or its equivalent)	121	67%	49%
College or vocational training	121	38%	21%
Ever detained or arrested	121	31%	51%
Females only: teen pregnancies, per 100	49	64	117
Functional competence (APL Survey: possible score 40)	109	24.6	21.8
% of years in special education	112	16%	28%

[a]Total n = 123

slightly over half of what they were for those who did not attend preschool. Preschool attendance led to a reduction of twenty percentage points in the detention and arrest rate and nearly that much in the high-school dropout rate. Those who attended preschool also did better on a test of functional competence.

These benefits considered in terms of their economic value make the preschool program a worthwhile investment for society. Over the lifetimes of the participants, preschool is estimated to yield economic benefits with an estimated present value that is over seven times the cost of one year of the program. The positive implications of these findings for improved quality of life for participating individuals, their families, and the community at large are of enormous importance.

YPSILANTI: AN OVERVIEW

The municipality of Ypsilanti was founded in 1823 as a trading post community called Woodruff's Grove. Commemorating its 150th year, the Supervisor of Ypsilanti Township wrote, "In the past century and a half, Ypsilanti has grown from a backwoods outpost on the midwestern frontier to a thriving center where education, commerce, and industry work hand in hand in the best interest of the community." The dual importance of the auto industry and educational institutions is reflected in Ypsilanti's motto: "Where commerce and education meet."

As a neighbor of Detroit, Ypsilanti understandably has a pattern of development that has been affected by the automotive and related industries ever since the first Ford plant was opened at the beginning of the century. In the two decades of the Perry Preschool study, growth in Ypsilanti (city and township) has been steady. The population has gone from 46,907 to 78,546—an increase of 67 percent. Until recently, local employment rates have also been steady; however, the early 1980s have been characterized by massive layoffs in the auto industry, leading to increases in unemployment rates.

Other local industries not associated with automotive manufacturing include paper products and stove production. Altogether, as of 1980, Ypsilanti had seventy-five industries employing over 24,000 workers.

Educationally, Ypsilanti has an active public school system as well as three institutions of higher learning. Approximately 7,400 pupils attend its nine elementary schools, two middle schools, and one high school. In light of the current publicity about the decline of our nation's schools, it is noteworthy that President Reagan in 1983 praised the Ypsilanti community for tightening its high-school graduation requirements.

A black community first began forming in Ypsilanti in the early 1850s, when the city was a stop on the underground railroad for escaped slaves traveling north as far as Canada. There were two stations in Ypsilanti, including one at the home of George McCoy, a black man who fled from slavery in Kentucky and settled in the city. McCoy made cigars and transported them in a wagon with a false bottom, which he used to hide fugitive slaves. With limited employment opportunities, the black community in Ypsilanti remained small until the arrival of the automobile industry some 50 years later. Today, blacks make up 20 percent of Ypsilanti's population.

EDUCATION

Ypsilanti schools have never been deliberately segregated, but because of housing patterns before 1960, the schools on the south side (Harriet School, later Perry) had few white children. The few blacks living in other parts of the city attended neighborhood schools along with their white peers. The major effect of the 1954 U.S. Supreme Court decision (Brown vs. the Board of Education) was on black teachers in Ypsilanti rather than directly on the pupils. Up until that time, all the black teachers had been at Perry School or in Special Education Services. After the Supreme Court's decision, however, black teachers were hired at other elementary schools as well as at the high school.

The 1950s were also a time when blacks first became active on the local school board. In 1953, Dr. Lawrence C. Perry (a black dentist and the namesake of Perry School) was elected to the board of education; he served two terms until his death in 1956. A black former city councilman, Amos Washington, was appointed to finish Dr. Perry's term; he was subsequently elected to the board of education on his own. Thus, in Ypsilanti as in the rest of the nation, the effects of the civil rights movement in the 1950s were being felt. Blacks not only elected two members to the city council, but were also beginning to enter the political world of the educational community.

Blacks active on the educational scene were concerned about reducing the large numbers of high school dropouts. A.P. Marshall, Ypsilanti historian, recalls the tremendous dropout rate in the 1940s and the early 1950s. There was employment available to uneducated youngsters in the plants but "also part of the reason had to be lack of emphasis or guidance on the part of parents." In the 1950s, while there was still high employment, "people began to look beyond what they were doing, beyond the bomber plant or the automobile factory, and to look at their opportunities." Marshall believes that this change in attitude prompted many black parents to encourage their youngsters to stay in school, and the percentage of those graduating began to increase.

Eugene Beatty, himself an educator, had a complementary and very personal perspective on the problem of black youngsters dropping out of high school. Beatty became the first black principal of Perry School in 1940. He recalls that at that time, no more than two black students graduated from Ypsilanti High School each year. Beatty attributes this to a lack of incentive to graduate—there were no black teachers in the high school to motivate and encourage black pupils. So, working at the elementary level, Beatty began promoting the value of education with his students and their parents. In 1947, he staged the first "elementary school graduation ceremony" for his 48 sixth graders; by the mid-1950s, 45 of the 48 students in that graduation class had completed high school in Ypsilanti, Willow Run, or other places to which they had moved. Beatty instituted other changes during his tenure as principal at Perry School. He made the school operate more like a community center, enabling the people to use the building for a variety of recreational and organizational functions. Thus, Beatty sent out a message that the school, like the church, could serve as a focal point for the black community.

Myrne Howe, a white teacher, taught black students at one of Ypsilanti's junior high schools in the 1950s. Her perspective on education is interesting in that it agrees with both Marshall's observations on the importance of parents and Beatty's emphasis on supportive role models in the schools. Howe in 1953 stated, "When parent-teacher conferences were first initiated, there was poor attendance due to unfamiliarity with the plan. However, now 85 percent or more of the parents attend." Yet Howe laments that only about half of the blacks entering high school will graduate, that only half of the graduates will go on to college, and that of those entering college perhaps only 20 percent will complete their studies.

While the situation has improved in the twenty years since Howe's observations, Ypsilanti still has a high dropout rate when compared with the rest of Washtenaw County and the State of Michigan (data obtained from "Dropout Rates," July 18, 1983). Statewide, school dropout rates are falling; from 1979-80 to 1980-81 the rate decreased from 6.5 percent to 5.6 percent. The present county rate of 4.5 percent is even lower than the state average. Ypsilanti, however, while following the downward trend, still shows a dropout rate of 13.1 percent (down from 15.7 percent in 1979-80). And though city statistics are not broken down by race, state figures show that dropout rates are much higher among blacks and Hispanics.

In sum, the twenty years during which the children of the Perry sample grew up saw significant change for Ypsilanti's black community, as did the rest of the nation. It was a time of expanding options in the areas of business, living conditions, political involvement, and educational advancement. Yet, as the most recent economic crisis in the nation has emphasized, opportunities for the poor black community have always lagged far behind the rest of America. Statistics on unemployment and school dropout rates show the continued vulnerability of black youth in today's society. The lives of several of the study's black youngsters, as outlined in the vignettes found in the pages that follow, illustrate the striking differences in the ways the youngsters responded to their circumstances and used the opportunities available to them.

SELECTING CHILDREN FOR THE STUDY

The children in the study lived in a neighborhood on the south side of Ypsilanti, Michigan, that was the attendance area of the Perry Elementary School. This area was (and is) an enclave of low-income black families. Children of preschool age were located for the study by identifying them on a Perry Elementary School census of families with youngsters attending the school, by referrals from neighborhood groups, and by door-to-door canvassing. Once children were identified as possibilities, their families were screened for socioeconomic level, which was computed on the basis of parents' scholastic attainment, the father's or single parent's level of employment, and the ratio of rooms to persons in the household. Children from families below a certain socioeconomic level were given the Stanford-Binet Intelligence Test. Children with IQ's between 60 and 90, with no evidence of organic handicap, were selected for the study.

Families whose children participated in the study were considerably less well-off than most children in the country, as reflected by comparisons with the U.S. Census. The parents had a median 9.4 years of schooling as the study began, only .4 years less than the national average for blacks in 1970, but 2.6 years less than the national average for all races. Fewer than one in five of the parents had completed high school, compared with national rates of one in three for blacks and one in two for all races. Forty-seven percent of the children in the study lived in single-parent families, compared with 14 percent for all races nationally. Residences were typical of local urban areas in size (median of 4.8 rooms), but were crowded, with more than twice the number of people in the typical household in the 1970 Census (6.7 vs. 2.7).

The available evidence indicates that these early conditions were persistent and that they were predictive of scholastic failure and other problems. In a parent survey eleven years after project entry (1973-1977), it was again found that in two out of five families, no parent was employed. Scholastic achievement scores at age fourteen for those who had not attended preschool averaged at the third percentile on national norms; and the high school dropout rate for this group was 42 percent, as compared with national rates for eighteen- to twenty-four-year-olds of 30 percent for blacks and nearly 18 percent for whites (National Center for Educational Statistics, 1982).

ASSIGNMENT TO GROUPS

The scientific strength of this study, its ability to determine preschool effects twenty years afterwards, is due primarily to an experimental design in which study subjects were randomly assigned to a group that went to preschool or to a group that did not go to preschool. Each year over a span of five school years (1962-67), children in the wave for that year were assigned to either one of two groups by forming pairs of children with similar pretest IQ's and assigning, at random, each pair member to one of the two groups. Then, pairs of similarly ranked children were exchanged between groups to equate within-group ratios of boys to girls and the average socioeconomic levels of the two groups. By flipping a coin, one group was assigned to the preschool condition and the other to the no-preschool condition. In Waves Two, Three, and Four, any siblings were assigned to the same group as their older siblings, to maintain the independence of the groups. Five children with single parents employed outside the home had to be transferred from the preschool group to the no-preschool group because of their inability to participate in the classroom and/or home-visit components of the preschool program. Once children were assigned to the groups, none of the families withdrew from the program. Clearly, neither teachers nor parents had influence in deciding who participated in the preschool program and who did not.

By these procedures, fifty-eight children were assigned to the preschool group, also called the experimental group; and sixty-five children were assigned to the no-preschool group, also called the control group.

Eleven years later, there were no differences between groups on demographic measures, such as father's presence or absence, father's employment, household density, neighborhood ratings by parents, and number of family moves since the child started school. Also, there was no difference between groups in maternal employment, with 27 percent employed in the preschool group versus 26 percent in the no-preschool group.

THE PRESCHOOL PROGRAM

The preschool program to which the fifty-eight children in the preschool group were assigned was an organized educational program directed at the intellectual and social development of young children. Each year it was staffed by teaching teams of four teachers who received extensive managerial supervision and inservice training. Children participated in the program for two school years at ages three and four, except in the case of the Wave Zero preschool group that received the program for one school year at age four. The school year began in October and ended in May, a relatively short 7½ month period. Classes were conducted for 2½ hours each morning Monday through Friday; the staff-child ratio was one adult for every five or six children enrolled. Teachers made a home visit to each mother and child for 1½ hours weekly.

Participation or nonparticipation in the preschool education program was the extent of differential treatment of members of the sample by the investigators. All participants in the study received the schedule of tests and interviews regardless of which group they were in. Testers, interviewers, and subsequent teachers were not informed by the investigators concerning the group membership of study participants.

EFFECTS ON SCHOOL SUCCESS

The conceptual framework of the study postulated that preschool education leads to greater school success and through school success, to greater socioeconomic success and increased social responsibility.

Preschool led to greater school success for study subjects. The finding of school success through late adolescence is consistent with results reported for earlier ages, extending further in time and to broader domains. Improvement in the school performance of children who attended preschool is indicated by higher achievement test scores, by higher grade-point averages, and by lower numbers of failing marks. Greater parental satisfaction with how children have done in school is also viewed as indicative of greater school success. Greater commitment to schooling is reflected in more favorable attitudes toward high school, as well as in early evidence of reduced absences and of improvement in attitudes and behavior. Improved school placement is shown by a decrease in the proportion of time that individuals spent receiving special education services, and a decline in the number of persons classified by the school as mentally retarded. Higher educational attainment is indicated by more persons graduating from high school and by more persons pursuing college or vocational training after high school graduation. Finally, substantial reductions in per-pupil costs of elementary and secondary education are obtained, primarily as a result of the reduced need for special education.

Success in school, as a concept, includes improved academic achievement, changes in student attitudes and behaviors, and changes in attitudes and behaviors of teachers. Together, these lead to changes in student placements. Success at this age also includes special achievements in other life areas distinct from school—in sports, community life, family and social relations, employment and income.

SCHOOL PERFORMANCE AND ATTITUDES

Evidence that the children attending preschool had a more positive school success flow is available from the earliest years of formal schooling.

Preschool education improved children's intellectual performance during the period from preschool through first grade. Intellectual performance was assessed by IQ tests. Contrary to initial expectations based on early IQ changes, IQs of the experimental and control group children were equivalent by second grade and remained so thereafter.

Study participants who attended preschool showed increased commitment to schooling through fifteen years of age (and subsequently at nineteen years as well). During elementary school, their teachers rated them higher than their no-preschool counterparts in academic motivation; when they were interviewed at age fifteen, they placed a higher value on schooling, had higher aspirations for college, showed greater willingness to talk to their parents about school, spent more time on their homework, and rated themselves more highly on school ability.

Preschool education led to improved scholastic placement, as shown by a decreased rate of placement in special education classes. Preschool education contributed to increased scholastic achievement during the years of elementary and middle school, as measured by standardized achievement tests. At age fourteen, the average achievement test score of those youths who had attended preschool was 1.2 grade-equivalent units higher than the average score of those who had not attended preschool; significant differences between groups occurred not only for overall achievement but also for reading, language, and arithmetic subtests.

The improved school success of children who attended preschool was also evident to their parents, who reported greater satisfaction with the school performance of their children. In parent interviews, 51 percent of parents of fifteen-year-olds who had attended preschool said their children had done as well in school as they would have liked, while only 28 percent of parents of those who had not attended preschool said this.

Preschool education contributed to improvements in academic performance in elementary, middle, and secondary school. The youths who had attended preschool had better marks through secondary school. School records were sufficiently complete to yield high school grade-point averages for 64 percent of the study sample; the control group had a C– average, while the group attending preschool had slightly better than a C average. Similarly, individuals who attended preschool had fewer failing grades, on the average, in both elementary and secondary school.

EFFECTS ON SCHOOL PLACEMENT AND EXPERIENCES

Preschool education led study participants to have different school experiences. It led the preschool group to fewer absences, and, more significantly, it reduced the incidence, time spent in, and level of special education services.

During elementary school, individuals who had attended preschool had, on the average, fewer absences per year than those who had not attended preschool—twelve days versus sixteen days per year.

Those persons who had attended preschool spent fewer of their school years in special education—that is, in integrated (mainstreamed) or self-contained classrooms after being classified as handicapped. Even among individuals receiving special education services, the mean number of years spent in special education was significantly lower. For those who had gone to preschool and were later classified as handicapped, the average time spent in special education was about 5½ years, whereas for those who had not gone to preschool the average time spent was almost 7¼ years. The proportion of persons ever classified as mentally retarded was much lower for those who had attended preschool: 15 percent compared with 35 percent for those who had not been to preschool. This reduction takes on special meaning if one bears in mind that participants were initially selected for the study on the basis of low IQ (among other factors), which is usually an indication of high vulnerability to placement in special education.

When other special services are considered in addition to special education—compensatory and remedial education, as well as early speech and language support—a somewhat different picture emerges. It is of special interest that children who went to preschool spent more time receiving remedial education. The contrast is suggestive: Children who attended preschool were more often classified as in need of remedial support, whereas those who did not were more frequently classified as mentally retarded. A possible explanation is that children who have gone to preschool appear to their teachers in the early elementary grades to have more academic promise, more potential, than do those who have not attended preschool; with a little help, the former could perform well in school, while the latter require more extreme measures. In fact, teacher ratings of the two groups of children in early elementary school show just that: Teachers rated children who had been to preschool, on the average, as showing more academic potential and motivation than children who had not gone to preschool.

EFFECTS ON EDUCATIONAL ATTAINMENT

Two out of three individuals who attended preschool graduated from high school; the comparable rate for persons in our sample who had not attended preschool was one out of two. Educational attainment is summarized in Table 2; High school graduation is very much the "bottom line" of school success at this age, and it is a necessary step for continuing education. Although age nineteen is too early to confidently estimate the ultimate educational attainment of study subjects, failing to graduate from high school presents a significant obstacle to future educational progress. Graduation is also an important consideration, if not an absolute prerequisite, for many jobs or opportunities for vocational training.

Preschool helped study participants overcome some of the disadvantages of coming from lower-income families and of being more educationally vulnerable than the national black population. The percent of high school graduates in the study sample can be compared to national figures. In 1980 in the United States, sixty-six percent of all blacks aged nineteen and twenty graduated from high school or received a graduate equivalency diploma, while for the study's control group, the rate was forty-nine percent and for the experimental group, sixty-seven percent. Preschool thus raised the rate of graduation to the national level for blacks.

Persons who attended preschool were more likely to have enrolled in some form of further education or vocational training after graduating from high school. If we consider either academic or vocational training, Table 2 shows that the group who had been to preschool had a nonsignificantly higher percent of persons in each of these categories. However, the difference between groups reached statistical significance when both categories were considered together: thirty-eight percent of those who had attended preschool undertook further education or training, as compared with twenty-one

Table 2 EDUCATIONAL ATTAINMENT

Category	National Data	Preschool ($n = 58$)	No-Preschool ($n = 63$)
Blacks graduating from high school	66%	67%	49%
Receiving postsecondary academic training	25%	19%	13%
Receiving postsecondary vocational training	13%	19%	10%
Receiving either academic or vocational training	n/a[a]	38%	21%[b]

(a) n/a means not applicable.

(b) Figures for "Receiving either academic or vocational training" may be less than the sum of academic and vocational categories, since a person might receive both kinds of training. See text for definition of categories.

percent of those who had not attended preschool. Precisely comparable national figures on postsecondary education or training rates are not available; however, in 1980 the proportion of blacks aged 19 and 20 in college was 25 percent, versus 13 percent for our study's control group; and the proportion of blacks aged 18 to 24 in postsecondary vocational programs was 13 percent, as compared with 10 percent for our control group. To the extent that these two national figures from different sources can be compared, it can be seen that preschool raised the rates of postsecondary education and training of the preschool group to approximately the national levels for blacks.

AN ECONOMIC ANALYSIS OF PRESCHOOL'S EFFECTS

In this section, we will examine the reductions in costs to the elementary and secondary education system related to preschool attendance. Our analysis is limited because study participants have not necessarily completed their education by age nineteen. Thus, we examine in this section the reductions in cost associated with differences in educational attainment only through the end of high school.

Putting a child who went to preschool through elementary and secondary school cost the school system, on the average, $34,813 (in constant 1981 dollars); putting one who did not attend preschool through elementary and secondary school cost, on the average, $41,895. The difference is $7,082 per child; that is, preschool reduced the cost of elementary and secondary education by $7,082 per child. Since preschool also increased the average educational attainment, this cost difference understates the total increase in educational efficiency.

The effects of preschool on the efficiency of the school production process can be estimated more precisely by calculating the average cost per year of school attainment in both groups. The decrease in cost per year attained that is attributable to preschool is $800. In other words, preschool reduced the cost per student of successfully completing each additional year of school from $3,930 to $3,130; this difference corresponds to a little over twenty percent of the annual cost of elementary and secondary education without preschool. Thus we can say that preschool increased the efficiency of the educational process by about twenty percent.

These reductions come about in two ways: Proportionately fewer children who attended preschool were in special education, and those who were in special education received fewer years of service. This is particularly true for children classified by the school system as educable mentally retarded. Furthermore, reductions in per-child costs between the two groups occurred in spite of the fact that persons who attended preschool have gone to school longer—a situation that tends to raise the costs of education for the study's experimental participants.

These findings are highly encouraging. However, they require some further elaboration. In economic analyses, the timing of costs and of cost reductions must be taken into account as well as their magnitude. A dollar today or in the near future is worth more than a dollar many years from now. To take into account the timing of costs and benefits, we convert all dollar figures to their discounted present value. The discounted present value of the $7,082 difference in total educational costs is $5,113 per child, using a discount rate of three percent. The amount of $5,113 is greater than the present value of the cost of one year of preschool.

Cost reductions reflect only part of preschool's effect on education; preschool also increased educational attainment. If this is taken into account, the effect of preschool on costs per year attained is greater than the effect of preschool on total educational costs (nineteen percent instead of fifteen percent). Thus preschool is an even better investment in terms of educational returns than the difference in total costs indicates.

SUMMARY: COST EFFECTIVENESS

Early education can lead to increased school success. In the Perry Preschool study, persons who had attended preschool had better grades, fewer failing marks, and fewer absences in elementary school; they required fewer special education services, were more likely to graduate from high school, and were more likely to continue their education or get vocational training after school than their no-preschool counterparts. The picture of detailed and consistent improvement in school performance and placement is also reflected in increased commitment: Those youths who attended preschool had a more favorable attitude toward high school. The economic analysis of these findings indicates that early education can substantially increase the efficiency of later schooling and that the effect of preschool education on school system costs alone is sufficient to cover the costs of early education.

Thus, preschool programs can substantially increase the efficiency of elementary and secondary education, not only by reducing costs but also by increasing effectiveness. In addition to reducing costs, preschool will boost the school performance of children who have a relatively poor prognosis for school success. These children put more into education (school commitment) and they get more out (school achievement, educational attainment). On a large scale, improving the educational process for disadvantaged children seems likcly to benefit all students by raising the average level of commitment and achievement in the environment in which education takes place.

EFFECTS ON SOCIAL RESPONSIBILITY

Preschool led study subjects to greater social responsibility. The preschool group had lower crime rates and less delinquent behavior than the no-preschool group, as indicated by fewer arrests, fewer cases sent on to juvenile court, fewer months on probation, and fewer persons fined as adults. Fewer pregnancies and births through age nineteen were reported by females in the study's preschool group. In the economic analysis, significant per-group cost savings have accrued because of reduced criminal justice system and victim costs resulting from reductions in crime.

As young people reach adulthood, they enter several arenas

that require them to assume new roles and responsibilities. Forming permanent relationships and raising children, moving away or staying at home, becoming involved with local churches and associations, voting—these new arenas are important because they offer young adults opportunities to make choices that have significant and long-lasting consequences.

Four aspects of social responsibility are examined: (1) involvement with the legal system; (2) formation of new family linkages and relations with the family of origin; (3) relations with neighbors and community groups; (4) other personal and social characteristics. Involvement with the legal system was assessed by examining participants' responses to interview questions on this subject and by examination of police and court records. The formation of new family linkages and relations with the family of origin were assessed by obtaining information on whether or not subjects were living at least part of the time at home; their attitudes toward the family, their family's attitudes toward them; their pregnancies and number of children, if any; and their marital status or living-together arrangements. Relations with neighbors and community groups were assessed by examining subjects' formal links with community institutions, organizations, and clubs; by analyzing subjects' responses to questions about involvement in activities "for others"; and by examining subjects' voter registration and voting records. Other personal and social characteristics were assessed by examining the results of measures of self-esteem, subjects' perceptions of their health and illnesses, and their reported use of leisure time.

Evidence showing that preschool led to a reduction in antisocial behavior and misconduct is available from our study of the preschool group during their elementary school years and also at age 15. For example, elementary school teachers rated children who had attended preschool as having better classroom conduct and personal behavior than their no-preschool counterparts. Preschool was associated with a reduction in the frequency with which age-fifteen study participants reported being kept after class. Preschool also led to reductions in the frequency of self-reported misbehavior and delinquent behavior at age fifteen. The proportion of persons who had reported none or one offense was higher for the preschool group: forty-three percent as compared with twenty-five percent for those with no preschool. There were fewer persons in the preschool group than in the no-preschool group with five or more offenses (twenty-five percent vs. fifty-two percent). When delinquent behaviors involving violence or theft were weighted according to seriousness, a similar difference was found.

The preschool group had fewer contacts with the criminal justice system than did the no-preschool group, including fewer arrests. This finding applies both when we look at each wave of subjects as they reached age nineteen and when we look at the complete sample through mid-1982, when the subjects ranged in age from nineteen to twenty-four years.

The estimated present value of preschool's total benefit to society as a result of reduced crime is just over $3,100 per child. This present value estimate is quite probably low because it understates victim costs; more important, it is also quite likely to be low because noneconomic factors are not included. Much of the cost of crime to its victims is not expressible with any accuracy in dollars, since it also includes the factors of mental anguish, and physical suffering; if monetary equivalents of these factors were to be provided, the benefit of reduction in crime would far exceed $3,100. There are also nonvictim benefits that are not included: The quality of life for persons who are not involved in crime (but might have been) has been improved. There is also a psychological benefit to people generally from reduced fear of crime, and there are reduced public and private crime prevention costs that accompany a general reduction in crime rates. Finally, even if all victim costs are excluded from consideration, the benefit to society simply from reductions in criminal justice system costs is almost $2,300.

LONG TERM IMPACT

The question of the effectiveness of early childhood education for children of low-income families has been investigated by dozens of social scientists over the past two decades. This chapter summarizes what is known about the effectiveness of early childhood education by analyzing the results of several of these longitudinal evaluations.

In the early 1960s many leading educators and social scientists suggested that preschool education for poor children was a way to break the cycle of poverty, assuming a chain of cause and effect that linked family poverty to children's scholastic failure and subsequent poverty as adults. Their suggestions eventually led to the establishment in the summer of 1965 of the national Head Start program. Speculation was that providing preschool education for poor children would enhance their intelligence. This theory received support from early reports that several experimental preschool programs were in fact raising IQ's.

However, in 1969 the oft-cited negative evaluation of Head Start by Westinghouse Learning Corporation and Ohio University was released. It diminished President Nixon's support for the program and was also largely responsible for the widespread and incorrect belief, still held by some today, that Head Start was a failure. Henry Levin's 1977 statement is typical of the tone of the times: "Good [preschool] programs are able to produce salutary increases in IQ for disadvantaged children, but these improvements are not maintained when the children enter the primary grades."

As the years went by, however, evidence of preschool's effectiveness began to mount. Evidence from several evaluations demonstrated that good preschool programs have both short- and long-term positive effects on low-income subjects. Seven of these evaluations are considered, including the Perry Preschool study. These seven studies are frequently associated with the research scientists, typically educational or developmental psychologists, who initiated them. Susan Gray's Early Training study and David Weikart's Perry Preschool study began in 1965. In 1966, Francis Palmer began the Harlem study. Also in 1966, Eleanor Monroe and M.S. McDonald of the Rome, Georgia, school system began that town's Head Start program on which they would conduct a follow-up study in 1981. Rick Heber and Howard Garber initiated the Milwaukee study in 1968. In 1975 the New York

Department of Education began an evaluation of its Experimental Prekindergarten program under the direction of David Irvine. This statewide program was established by the New York State Legislature in 1966 and now receives about $10 million a year in state funding. This evaluation helped persuade New York Education Commissioner Gordon Ambach to make his widely reported statement in 1983 that children should begin school at age four.

THE NATURE OF PRESCHOOL'S EFFECTIVENESS

What does the research tell us about the effectiveness of early childhood education? The most far-reaching lesson is that the impact of early childhood education can extend to adulthood. The difficulties of longitudinal research have caused some to doubt this fact. Some researchers have spoken resignedly of the "temporal erosion" of program effects. But we have found that the positive impact of programs of high quality endures; it is just the manifestations of this impact that change as people mature and move into new settings. This is not to say that a preschool program, by itself, can eliminate the effects of poverty. A person's life is not transformed in some magical way by experience in a preschool program. But a successful preschool experience can permanently alter the success/failure trajectory of a person's life in significant and very positive ways.

Several stages of development converge to make the preschool age an opportune time for intervention. Physically, the young child has matured to the point that he or she has achieved both fine- and gross-motor coordination and is able to move about easily and freely. Mentally, the child has developed basic language capabilities and can use objects for self-chosen purposes. In the terms of Jean Piaget, the child has shifted from sensory-motor functioning to preoperational capacity. Socially, the child is able to move away from familiar adults and social contexts, into new settings. The fear of strangers, so common earlier, is gone, and the youngster welcomes relations with new peers and adults.

When we look at the basic accomplishments of early education, what stands out is that the child develops new competencies related to emerging social and physical skills and intellectual thought. Armed with these new competencies, the child
learns to relate to new adults who respond to his or her
performance very differently from the family. In short, the
child learns to demonstrate new abilities in new settings and
to trust new adults and peers enough to display these skills
willingly. The child's willingness to try new things and develop new competencies is the seed that is transformed into
later school and life success.

QUALITY: THE KEY TO PRESCHOOL'S LONG-TERM EFFECTIVENESS

The development of programs of high quality is a priority
for those dedicated to delivering on the promise of such child
care and education projects as the Perry Preschool Project. It
is not easy, however, to meet the challenge. It is entirely
possible for staff to operate early education programs in such
a manner that the outcomes described in this report are not
achieved.

What are the elements necessary to produce a program of
high quality? The National Association for the Education of
Young Children (1983) has proposed a list of criteria, covering
ten areas, deemed essential for program success. These areas
are physical environment, health and safety, nutrition and
food service, administration, staff qualifications and development, staff-parent interaction, staff-child interaction, child-
child interaction, curriculum, and evaluation. These criteria—
the consensus of expert opinion, practice, and research
—provide a useful base for judging programs. In our opinion,
however, programs could meet many of these criteria and still
not be of high quality.

Such criteria are the basis for standards and licensing
requirements in many states; they are necessary, but not
sufficient, to maintain a high quality program. Style of program operation is the additional ingredient necessary to ensure high quality. The style in which a program is operated is

manifested in the skillful blending of program elements, such as those described above. Elements of particular importance are as follows: curriculum implementation, parent involvement, staff supervision, inservice training provision, teacher planning time, staff relationships, ongoing evaluation, and administrative leadership. These elements are not rigidly tied to a "right" way of doing things; for example, it is not as important which curriculum is chosen, as that a curriculum model is chosen to guide program operations.

School Success from an Early Start

Bonita has a bachelor's degree in special education; she plans to obtain her master's degree and then teach. By her own account, school has always been an avenue of success for her. Bonita's father attributes at least some of his daughter's initial academic success to the early start she got through her preschool involvement: "I think it was the right help because she learned how to do a lot of the things when she got into kindergarten; see, they gave her a jump." When she, herself, becomes a teacher, Bonita believes it will be her job to challenge the intellectual capacity of each of her young pupils; she does not believe that the easy way out results in any lasting academic gains: "I know it's a lot of work and it's much harder, but I think maybe they would get more out of their education."

—from Bonita Emerson: A Case Study

WHO PROFITS MOST FROM A GOOD
PRESCHOOL PROGRAM?

The number of three- and four-year-olds enrolled in early childhood education programs, excluding custodial day care, increased from 1.5 to 2.6 million between 1970 and 1985. The largest percentage increase of all three- and four-year-olds enrolled in such programs took place between 1965 and 1985, rising from 10.6 to 37 percent. There are more early childhood educators as well. Membership in the National Association for the Education of Young Children has increased by 10,000 persons in the past six years, to a total of over 38,000 members in 1983.

Even as many parents are deciding that their children should receive early childhood education, we are compelled to ask, on the basis of the research reviewed here, which children benefit most from early childhood programs? The research presented here applies directly to children who live in poverty and to handicapped children. In addition, we see a need to serve the children of women who work outside the home, particularly children in single-parent families whose mothers have low-paying jobs.

Children who live in poverty. The risk of educational failure falls heavily on children who live in poverty. Their families are not able to pay for early education services. Of the 20.3 million youngsters aged five and under in this country in 1982, twenty-two percent lived in poverty—4.5 million children (U.S. Bureau of the Census, 1982b). In 1986, according to The Children's Defense Fund, more than one of every four children under age six live in poverty, as do more than half the children in households headed by women. In spite of our national efforts, including Head Start, the economically disadvantaged are underserved: 81 percent of three-year-olds and 61 percent of four-year-olds from families with incomes under $10,000 were not enrolled in an early childhood education program in 1980. Today, only eighteen percent of the children eligible for participation in Head Start are actually served by it.

Handicapped children. There is evidence that early education helps children at risk of later placement in special education. The Perry Preschool study documented effects for youngsters who tested as borderline mentally retarded. Another study found that trainable mentally retarded children profited from at least two years of preschool (Moore, Fredericks, and Baldwin, 1981). Other studies have found short-term benefits for children with sensory impairments, language problems, and behavior disorders (U.S. Bureau of Education for the Handicapped, 1976); and Down's Syndrome (Ludlow and Allen, 1979; Maisto and German, 1979; Simeonsson, Cooper, and Scheiner, 1982).

Many believe that the handicapped, those who need special

School: Passing Through and Hanging Out

Although Yvonne has graduated from high school, her records are dotted with academic problems and disciplinary incidents from the time she entered kindergarten. She summarizes her school experiences as follows: "When I was coming up in school I should have knew what I wanted to do because now I kind of regret being bad in school and hanging out. . . ." A series of offenses—smoking in the bathroom, fighting with peers, arguing with teachers—resulted in a total of three suspensions and two expulsions. Academically, Yvonne coasted through school, just getting by: "I passed through, but I also did a lot of hanging out. I was skipping all the time, I'd do my work, I passed. . . . You know, I do my work and then after I got the grade for that one semester, or that week, then I knew it would be time to hang out." She showed interest in sports and music in school, but never made these interests lead to anything; even today she expresses regret at the missed opportunities: "Well, I messed up in high school when I had a chance to be on the basketball team and try to do something for myself or make it to somebody's college or whatever. I was hanging out a lot, you know, just messing around, and I didn't accomplish what I wanted to, see, and I'm still mad at myself about that."

—*from Yvonne Barnes: A Case Study*

---

educational services, deserve priority in receiving early childhood services. In the 1981-82 school year there were nearly 228,000 children aged three to five receiving special education services through Public Law 94-142 (U.S. Office of Special Education and Rehabilitative Services, 1983). By 1984, the

number of Special Education youngsters served by Head
Start had risen to 60,000. Altogether, these numbers represent
only about half of all handicapped children in this age group.
Twenty-seven states have no legislation mandating the provision of educational services for handicapped children aged
five and under.

Children of women who work.   The number of women in the
labor force has grown rapidly in past decades, approaching 50
million. By 1985, according to the Department of Labor, 59.5
percent of the 6 million women with children between the ages
of three and five are in the labor force. A growing number of
mothers head single-parent families; there were 3.1 million
children under age five in such families in 1980, and the
number has been growing since. Many of these mothers have
taken low-paying jobs that have not really removed them from
the ranks of the poor. As these numbers grow, so does the
need for preschool programs and child care facilities.

There appears to be little reason to distinguish between
part-time preschool programs and full-time day-care programs as far as their potential benefits to preschool-aged
children. The Milwaukee Project certainly demonstrated that
a day-care program can contribute to children's future scholastic success. Similar evidence on the benefits of a comprehensive program comes from Craig Ramey's Abecedarian
Project at the University of North Carolina, Chapel Hill.

THE NEED TO REACH THE PUBLIC

Early childhood educators must communicate the importance of preschool education to the public. Most people are
not opposed to providing early childhood education of high
quality to those in need; they are simply unaware of its social
and economic justifications.

In seeking to communicate with the public, early childhood
advocates should start by contacting leaders who influence
public opinion and public policy. Early childhood advocates
can find leading citizens at meetings of various associations

and organizations. Business leaders can be reached at meetings of such clubs as the Rotary, Lions, and Optimists, as well as the Chamber of Commerce. Educators gather together at school board meetings and various associations of principals and teachers. Church groups should also be approached, in

---

Early Failure: Obstacles and Rescue

Marlene is being divorced after three years of marriage. She has two children, aged one and two, and is receiving Aid to Families with Dependent Children (AFDC) and food stamps. Marlene has never held a job. Before her marriage, she was enrolled in a secretarial program but dropped out after one year. Her future plans are vague and filled with excuses about the obstacles preventing her from achieving economic independence. Marlene talks about looking for a job—in the next breath saying why she cannot, or has not, done so: "I am going to try and find me a job; then I have to try and find me a babysitter. If I could get a job—but I haven't really had no transportation to go out there and look because our car's broke down on us—but as soon as I can get that opportunity to go look for a job, I am, because I need to get away from home to get my mind off things that are at home." The theme of escape from her troubles, even more than financial need, seems to be Marlene's primary motivation for wanting a job. Similarly, she sees finding a new mate as her means of rescue from her current situation. Marlene says she plans to find someone who will be better to her than her first husband and provide her with more money than she receives on public assistance.

—from Marlene Franklin: A Case Study

---

part because they either provide or house in their churches the greatest number of child care facilities in the country (Lindner, Mattis, and Rogers, 1983) and in part because many of the community's opinion leaders attend these groups' meetings. Political leaders, of course, meet regularly in national and state capitals, and in country, township, and city halls. Professional associations of physicians (especially pediatricians), lawyers, and social workers also meet regularly. Once these persons are aware of the value of individuals and to society of early childhood education of high quality, they will be much more likely to support such efforts.

The widespread establishment of early childhood programs of high quality in the United States can only be accomplished

---

School as a Place for Success

Outside of his family, Jerry sees three major influences that have played a role in setting his goals: friends, teachers, and his high school guidance counselor. Jerry's friendships seem to have been based on shared academic interests, with the students reinforcing in one another the importance of learning and accomplishing something. His mother recalls that Jerry primarily chose his friends from school and had a racially mixed peer group. Jerry also claims that his teachers always rewarded and encouraged his academic accomplishments, especially in his elementary school years. He says of them as a group: "I guess the teachers helped a lot. Back then, I'd put them first." And in high school, it was his senior counselor who became aware of Jerry's mathematical ability and encouraged him to go into engineering and drafting when he entered college. Without the influence of this counselor, says Jerry, "I would have ended up going to school, but not knowing what I was going for. I would just have been taking classes."

—from Jerry Andrews: A Case Study

---

with widespread public support. Certainly, key decisions, particularly about the national Head Start program, will continue to be made in Washington, D.C. We anticipate that other key decisions will be forthcoming in the next decade from state governments. In fact, state governments have the most to gain from the establishment of these programs, for it is state governments that now bear the vast costs of education (particularly for children from low-income families), of the legal system, and of the welfare system. Their initial financial outlays for provision of high quality early childhood programs for children from low-income families will, in the long run, result in savings in state budgets.

But there are thousands of decisions in thousands of other forums that will also affect the provision of high quality early childhood programs. Local school boards can commit local funds to such services whenever they choose to. One of the major expenditures, even now, of United Way and similar consolidated charities is for child care programs. Many corporations are now considering whether to provide early childhood programs for the children of their employees.

Most important of all, parents make decisions each day that directly affect the quality of life and the environment for learning and development of their young children. Parents must learn to accept only high-quality early childhood programs. Those who are able to must be willing to pay for this program quality. We must all join with those who cannot afford to pay, to make sure that such programs are available to their children, because, in the end, the nation wins as well as the children and families served.

THE CHALLENGE TO THE NATION

It is time for the nation to recognize the importance of early childhood education to the healthy development of its children. The research does not indicate that all programs produce outcomes such as those reported in the Perry Preschool study, or that all children who participate in such programs will obtain the same strong outcomes. But it does indicate that such programs, on the whole, can produce outcomes of value to both families and society.

The research findings of the Perry Preschool study and the others reported in *Changed Lives,* indicate that high quality early childhood programs for disadvantaged children produce long-term changes in their lives—changes that permit more education, training, and employment; less crime, delinquency, and welfare subsistence; and a lower birth rate for teenage mothers. These factors weave a pattern of life success that not only is more productive for children and their families but also produces substantial benefits to the society at large through reduction in taxpayer burden and improvement in the quality of community life.

Early childhood education is *not* a panacea, however. It does not solve the nation's unemployment problem. It does not solve the problem of how to deliver effective education in the elementary and high school years to the "graduates" of good early childhood programs. It does not solve the problem of inadequate housing. It does not solve the nation's crime problem. Early childhood education *does* give young children in need a firmer foundation on which to mature and prosper— an edge in opportunity and performance. It is *part* of the solution, not the *whole* solution.

The research demands prompt action to benefit the common good. We must get about the task.

THREE PRESCHOOL CURRICULUM MODELS: How Children are Affected

by Lawrence J. Schweinhart, David P. Weikart, and Mary B. Larner

When studies of the effects of early childhood education began in the 1960s, the basic question under investigation was, "Does early childhood education make a difference in the lives of children?" Fears at that time were that early education would be harmful to the development of children and their relationship with their families. The several longitudinal studies initiated in 1962 before the advent of Head Start, directed by Susan Gray, Martin Deutsch, and David Weikart, addressed this question by establishing designs in which experimental groups participated in preschool education and control groups did not. As these studies, and others such as

Starting in 1967, High/Scope president David Weikart and associates evaluated the long-term success of three different approaches to preschool learning. Though all three improved youngsters' cognitive skills, the effects on behavior varied widely. This report appeared in the Early Childhood Research Quarterly, Spring, 1986.

those included in the Consortium for Longitudinal Studies (1983), reported their long-term results, the answer to the basic question became clear. High quality early childhood education for disadvantaged children is a highly effective way of improving their life chances.

So it was found that early childhood education can work. High-quality programs for disadvantaged children, the ones most in need and most difficult to reach, can have positive effects. It is clear, however, from the data of the Perry Preschool study and others, that even highly effective programs will not *cure* the problems of all the children, their families, or of society—far broader efforts at social reform involving more than education alone are necessary for that end. Nevertheless, these findings do suggest a means for addressing problems at an early age.

As positive as these educational and social outcomes are, it is the cost information that has proven to be most persuasive to policymakers and citizens with long-range fiscal concerns. In the fall of 1985, the Research and Policy Committee of the Committee for Economic Development (CED) released a study of American education from the perspective of leaders of major corporations. In *Investing in Our Children* (1985), this body of corporate and education leaders stated:

> *If we examine the Perry Preschool Program for its investment return and convert all costs and benefits into current values based on a three percent real rate of interest, one year of the program is an extraordinary economic buy. It would be hard to imagine that society could find a higher yield for a dollar of investment than that found in preschool programs for its at-risk children.*

But there is a condition on this conclusion. The preschool programs that have demonstrated long-term effectiveness have been of *high quality*. It is precisely this issue of further defining program quality that the High/Scope Preschool Curriculum study and other preschool curriculum comparison studies have addressed.

THE THREE MODELS

The preschool curriculum models used in the project represented three theoretically distinct approaches to preschool programs.

(1) The programmed-learning approach, in which the teacher initiates activities and the child responds to them, was represented by the Distar direct-instruction preschool program developed by Carl Bereiter and Siegfried Engelmann (1966). In this approach, classroom activities are prescribed by behavioral sequences of stimuli, responses, and positive reinforcements. Objectives are clearly defined, usually pre-academic skills. The underlying psychological theory is behaviorist, as exemplified in the work of B. F. Skinner.

(2) The open-framework approach, in which teacher and child both plan and initiate activities and actively work together, was represented by the High/Scope Cognitively Oriented Preschool Curriculum (Hohmann, Banet, & Weikart, 1979). In this approach, classroom activities revolve around key experiences intended to promote intellectual and social development. The underlying psychological theory is cognitive-developmental, as exemplified in the work of Jean Piaget.

(3) The child-centered approach, in which the child initiates and the teacher responds, was represented by a nursery-school program that incorporated the elements of what has historically constituted good nursery-school practice. In this approach, classroom activities are the teacher's responses to the child's expressed needs and interests, and the teacher encourages children to actively engage in free play. Historically, the underlying psychological theory has been psychoanalytic, as exemplified in the work of Sigmund Freud.

The custodial-care approach was not represented in this study. In the custodial-care approach, both caregiver and child respond to events as they arise, and the caregiver's job is to keep children safe and out of trouble. Children watch television or engage in play without adult involvement. The custodial-care approach to preschool programs emphasizes their supervisory function to the exclusion of any planned educational activities or purpose and may be both appropriate and useful in the right circumstances.

COMMON CHARACTERISTICS OF THE PROGRAM

All three programs in the study were part of the same research project, with the same director, David Weikart, funding source, personnel policies, and position in the school system. All three programs in the study had two components—classroom sessions and educational home visits. Classroom sessions lasting 2½ hours were held five days a week, Monday through Friday. A teacher visited each mother and child at home in ninety-minute sessions every two weeks, during the part of the day when the class was not meeting. During the home visits, the teacher encouraged the mother to engage her child in learning activities that fit the curriculum approach used in that classroom.

Classes, operating between 1967 and 1970, consisted of either fifteen or sixteen three- and four-year-olds, with one exception: the 1969-70 open-framework class had thirteen children. Two teachers were assigned to each classroom group, making the typical ratio of teachers to children about one to eight. In addition, each classroom had an aide who also drove the bus; and, in each classroom, a female high-school special-education student was employed and received school credit to provide custodial care, particularly on bus rides to and from school and on field trips.

In the three years that the preschool programs were in operation, the six teacher positions were occupied by eleven women, most of them with masters' degrees in education, the others with bachelors' degrees in education. The aide remained the same for each curriculum model throughout the project. The open-framework and programmed-learning models were staffed by new teachers during the second year of the project; the programmed-learning model also replaced one teacher at the beginning of the third project-year. The teachers were all highly motivated to demonstrate that their curriculum model could be successful.

Each of the three teaching teams engaged in daily evaluation and planning sessions, reviewing activities and the progress of individual children, but the teams did not engage in joint planning or meetings. A staff supervisor provided guidance to all three teams and used the daily evaluation and planning sessions to help them maintain curriculum model goals and meet the needs of individual children. While it is possible that the director or supervisor could have exhibited subtle biases for or against a particular curriculum model, elaborate managerial procedures militated against it. After each home visit, the teacher completed a home-visit report, describing activities and evaluating child progress, and discussed these reports with the supervisor. Each program was frequently reviewed for faithfulness of curriculum implementation by nonteaching staff and outside consultants, who observed the classroom and met with the teachers and supervisor.

The teaching team implementing the Distar programmed-learning model received training from University of Illinois consultants trained and employed by the Bereiter-Engelmann curriculum-development team. The team implementing the High/Scope model engaged in the development of that model and continued to work with High/Scope curriculum consultants on further refinement. The team implementing the nursery-school model developed it themselves, drawing upon their early childhood education training, experience with children, and teacher intuitions, which are highly valued in this approach.

The programs were housed in two one-room country-school buildings within two miles of each other in Ypsilanti Township. During the first year of the project, one school building housed the open-framework model in the morning and the programmed-learning model in the afternoon, while the other school building housed the nursery-school program and the project administrative staff. During subsequent years, the open-framework and child-centered models operated in one school building, while the programmed-learning program operated in the other. This change was made because the programmed-learning model called for a setting with tables and chairs and no distractions, while the open-framework and child-centered models shared a need for abundant materials and equipment. Children attending each program rode separate buses to and from the preschool programs each day, so there was no contact between groups.

EFFECTS ON INTELLECTUAL PERFORMANCE

What can we learn from the comparison of the three different preschool program models with regard to children's intellectual performance over time? When the mean IQs of the three preschool curriculum groups are plotted separately, we see that the differences between them are quite small. During the first year of the preschool program, mean IQs, which ranged from 60 to 90 rose between 23 and 28 points, moving the groups of children out of the at-risk category. During the second preschool year, mean IQs of the open-framework and child-centered groups dropped 9 points, whereas that of the programmed-learning group dropped only 3 points and thereby achieved the only statistically significant advantage among groups at any testing. From the end of kindergarten onward, curriculum groups did not differ in mean IQs and stabilized in the range of 90 to 100. In contrast, the mean school-age IQ of the control group stabilized between 85 and 90.

The evidence indicates that preschool experience does indeed affect children's intellectual performance. The mean IQs achieved by preschool program participants stabilized at a higher level than those of a control group at six annual testings from ages four to ten.

The comparison of the three preschool curriculum models yielded scant evidence showing that the models were differentially effective in improving children's intellectual performance. The comparison of mean IQs showed that children from the programmed-learning model performed better than the other two groups at one testing, after two years of preschool experience. When all follow-up IQs (from ages four through ten) were averaged to give a mean IQ over time, the three preschool curriculum groups did not differ significantly: the programmed-learning group averaged 97, the open-framework group, 96, and the child-centered group 94.

EFFECTS ON SCHOOL ACHIEVEMENT

The only achievement scores gathered on all the children were the California Achievement Tests (CAT, lower primary form W) at the end of first and second grades. While each of the groups gained between fifty and sixty points between the two testings (using the same test form), the groups were not significantly different from one another at either time. This is to be expected, since the early IQ differences that separated the groups diminished by kindergarten and disappeared by the second grade. The modest early advantage that the programmed-learning group had over the other two was not translated into superior achievement in elementary school.

EFFECTS ON SOCIAL BEHAVIOR

Juvenile delinquency and other aspects of social behavior were examined for the Curriculum study sample by self-reports at age fifteen. According to these data, the programmed-learning group engaged in twice as many delinquent acts as did the other two curriculum groups, including five times as many acts of property violence and twice as many acts of drug abuse and such status offenses as running away from home. Other areas of social behavior corroborate this pattern of relatively poor social performance by the programmed-learning group—poor family relations, less participation in sports or school job appointments, lower expectations for educational attainment, and less reaching out to others for help with personal problems. For most of these variables, the sharpest contrast was with the open-framework group, whose social behavior was relatively positive. The curriculum groups performed similarly to each other in the spheres of employment and money, in measured self-esteem, and in perceived locus of control.

EFFECTS ON JUVENILE DELINQUENCY

The average member of the programmed-learning group engaged in thirteen self-reported delinquent acts, the child-centered group member, seven, and the open-framework group member, five. On all but one item of the eighteen-item scale the programmed-learning group reported the highest frequency or was tied for the highest frequency of the three groups.

The eighteen-item delinquency scale is divided into five subscales—personal violence, property violence, stealing, drug abuse, and status offenses. The programmed-learning group engaged in twice as many acts of personal violence as the other two groups, but this difference was not statistically significant because of the large variation among individuals within groups, particularly the programmed-learning group. The programmed-learning group had the highest frequencies of the three groups on each of the five items in that subscale.

The programmed-learning group engaged in five times as many acts of property violence as did the other two groups, reporting 1.7 acts per person as compared to only .3 acts per person in the other two groups. The programmed-learning group had the highest frequencies of the three groups on each of the three items in that subscale; the difference in the arson category was statistically significant. Groups did not differ significantly in frequencies reported for the stealing subscale. On four of the six items, the programmed-learning group reported slightly higher frequencies than the other two groups.

The programmed-learning group reported that they engaged in twice as many acts of drug abuse as did the other two groups, in use of both marijuana and other illegal drugs. The programmed-learning group reported that they engaged in twice as many activities that we have labeled "status offenses," exceeding the other two groups in fights with parents, trespassing, and, to a statistically significant extent, running away from home.

Curriculum groups at age fifteen did not yet manifest statistically significant differences in the official consequences of juvenile delinquency. Regardless of curriculum group, half the members of the sample reported having been picked up or arrested by police by age fifteen; the average sample member had been suspended from school 2.2 times.

Groups differed very little in numbers reporting five or fewer offenses, but eight (44 percent) out of eighteen members of the programmed-learning group—nearly half—engaged in sixteen or more delinquent acts, as compared to only three (8 percent) out of thirty-six members of the other two groups combined.

The one statistically significant group difference in the family domain was that one out of three members of the programmed-learning group said their families felt they were doing poorly, a response made by only one out of thirty-six members of the other two curriculum groups combined. Similarly, though not to a statistically significant extent, one out of five members of the programmed-learning group reported getting along poorly with their families, while no one in the open-framework group made this response. Finally, one out of three members of the open-framework group reported contributing to household expenses, while fewer than one out of six members of the programmed-learning group did so. Given the substantially higher rates of delinquent behavior reported by the programmed-learning group, their greater frequency of poor family relations should come as no surprise. On one other family-related matter, in this sample of fifty-four fifteen-year-olds, two persons reported having children of their own.

In social activities, the biggest group difference was in sports participation: nearly all of the open-framework group participated in sports, while fewer than half of the programmed-learning group did so. Compared to members of the programmed-learning group, twice as many members of the open-framework group had recently read a book. Groups were about the same in their participation in volunteer work—about one out of four sample members engaged in such activities.

No one in the programmed-learning group had ever been appointed to an office or special job at school. The strongest contrast here was with the child-centered group, which reported one out of three members with some school appointment. While this finding could be interpreted as reflecting the emphasis of the child-centered preschool curriculum on social development, it should be recalled that the child-centered group did enjoy certain socioeconomic advantages at project entry (for example, more highly educated mothers), and these advantages may have been responsible for the higher percentage receiving school appointments. Only half of the programmed-learning group expected to get any training beyond high school, while two thirds of the child-centered group and three quarters of the open-framework group expected to continue their education beyond high school.

Though the three curriculum groups reported about the same numbers of personal problems, the programmed-learning group members were least likely to seek help for their problems. Only two out of eighteen did so, as contrasted with seven out of eighteen in the open-framework group, a large though not statistically significant difference.

Curriculum groups showed no significant differences on a series of items reflecting their employment and financial affairs. At the age-fifteen interview, 26 percent of the sample members were working, and 61 percent had worked at some time. Eighty-three percent of them reported what work they hoped to have in their early twenties. Sixty-two percent of them had saved money, and 75 percent owned something worth more than twenty-five dollars.

The general picture that emerges at age fifteen is that, when compared to the other two groups, more of the programmed-learning group members reported that they were not socially well-adjusted. The programmed-learning group reported that they much more frequently engaged in all sorts of juvenile delinquent behavior, particularly offenses involving property damage and drug abuse, possibly reflecting lack of respect and even anger towards authority. More members of the pro-grammed-learning group reported poor family relations and were less likely to seek help for personal problems. The lesser degree of sports participation reported by the programmed-learning group suggests that its members were less likely than the members of the other two curriculum groups to seek or to receive social acceptance from either peers or teachers.

SUMMARY AND POLICY CONSIDERATIONS

When the High/Scope Preschool Curriculum study was established in 1967, the *most effective* preschool programs were thought to be those that espoused a structured curriculum. The structured curriculum has been interpreted by many educators to mean a didactic program with instructional "cookbooks" to aid teachers in remediating the difficulties learners encounter. Other approaches were thought to be not structured enough to achieve success. But we know that structured curriculum models can be diverse; for example, an open classroom can be highly, though subtly, structured if it is based on a rigorous theoretical model. The Curriculum study explored this issue by examining three theoretically diverse curriculum approaches.

In the monograph on the Curriculum study through age ten (Weikart et al., 1978), the startling conclusion was reached that insofar as we could measure intellectual and scholastic performance, all three preschool curriculum models appeared to achieve the same positive results. On the whole, the school-related results were better than those obtained with the experimental group of the Perry Preschool study by the same age. These findings of equivalence in intellectual and academic outcomes were surprising because the central issue in early childhood education has long been the selection of a curriculum. Advocates for various theoretical positions con-stantly argue about the needs of children and instructional goals from their theoretical perspective. The Curriculum study showed us that diverse curriculum models can be *equally* effective in improving children's education and that this success does not appear to derive from the curriculum models themselves, but rather from the way the programs are administered and operated.

The Curriculum study through age fifteen has produced two major findings. First, it has replicated the central finding of the Perry Preschool study and other studies in the Consortium for Longitudinal Studies (1983), demonstrating once again that high-quality preschool programs for poor children can lead to improvements in their intellectual and scholastic performance that last at least through age ten. This replicative finding is important because it takes at least ten years to conduct such a study.

Second, it has found significant differences at age fifteen in social-behavior outcomes among the groups experiencing the various preschool curriculum approaches. In this study, the group that received a preschool program using the teacher-directed programmed-learning approach, when compared to groups receiving preschool programs that encouraged children to initiate their own activities, evidenced substantially higher rates of self-reported juvenile delinquency and associated problems. Given that the youngsters in this study were only fifteen years old, and building on the findings of the Perry study at this age, we anticipate that the groups will continue their juvenile delinquency patterns in the coming years, making it likely that group differences in crime and delinquency will eventually be even larger.

The Curriculum study's most recent data suggest that there are important social consequences to preschool curriculum choices. In the earlier elementary-school years, trends that were not statistically significant foreshadowed these later findings. According to the ratings of first- and second-grade teachers, the programmed-learning group consistently was rated lower than the open-framework group on sociability, cooperation, and academic orientation.

There is no evidence here that youngsters in the programmed-learning group were worse off than they would have been if they had not attended the preschool program. Indeed, their self-reported juvenile delinquency pattern is much better than that of the Perry Preschool study control-group youngsters. The program's major goals were academic, not social. It is reasonable, therefore, to find few if any social-behavior effects, positive or negative. The point is that the other two preschool curriculum approaches in this study did have social-behavior goals and did appear to produce favorable long-term social effects signified by lower rates of juvenile delinquency and other social-behavior problems, as well as equivalent academic outcomes.

We can speculate about why social alienation occurred among such a substantial number of youths in the programmed-learning group. Apparently a preschool curriculum that emphasizes direct transmission of knowledge can be less successful in helping children adapt to the interpersonal realities of rules and conventions. The findings of the High/Scope Preschool Curriculum study prompt us to ask whether temporary intellectual advantages gained from a preschool program might sometimes be purchased at the price of deficits in social behavior.

Young children appear to learn from both their relationship to the teacher and peers and the manner in which knowledge is gained. While knowledge that young children gain in several curriculum approaches may appear to be the same as the knowledge that is dispensed *to* the child, the social consequences for the child may be very different.

For some years, we interpreted the findings of the High/Scope Preschool Curriculum study to imply that high-quality early childhood education could be built upon *any* theoretically coherent model. The High/Scope Preschool Curriculum study, with its age-fifteen data, no longer permits that conclusion. The latest interpretation from the study, tenuous though the data are, now must be that a high-quality preschool curriculum is based on child-initiated learning activities.

This report requires major restraint in its use and interpretation. These are the data that traditional early childhood educators have been predicting since journalist Maya Pines introduced the Bereiter-Englemann method to the world as a "pressure-cooker" approach in the mid-1960s. These are the findings that programmed-learning specialists have considered unlikely, because academic skill improvement was seen to promote self-esteem and adjustment to the real world. Actually, what these data add to the debate is a plea for caution. Its sample size, while carefully drawn and randomly assigned over a three-year period, is small. These findings must be replicated in other projects with good enough data to explore this issue. We do plan to collect data on the Curriculum study sample, as we did in the Perry study, in late adolescence after high school graduation, particularly data pertaining to delinquency and social behavior. These findings cannot be generalized to types of children who were not included in our sample, and it is clear that we studied poor children at risk of school failure.

While this one research study alone does not justify drawing policy implications, it does suggest some policy considerations. First, these results give pause to educators rushing to expand *formal* schooling down to age four. While good early-childhood programs are an effective way to improve the life chances of disadvantaged children, *formal academic* programs as represented by teacher-directed learning models may be inadequate to the task, because they fail to have the desired social-behavior consequences. Second, current uses of teacher-directed learning methods in early childhood care and education should be subjected to careful scrutiny and rigorous evaluation. We cannot continue to excuse an almost exclusive focus on the use of intellectual and academic measures for program effectiveness because measures of appropriate social competence are elusive. While it would be totally inappropriate, on the strength of this study alone, to suggest across-the-board curtailment of teacher-directed models in early education programs, the fact that academically oriented programmed-learning approaches may be ineffective in reducing children's later social-behavior problems should be carefully evaluated. Third, it is time to initiate longitudinal studies on the long-term effects of teacher- and child-initiated curriculum approaches in early childhood education. Additionally, opportunities should be aggressively explored to initiate studies to examine the issues raised by the Curriculum study. Fourth, like the field of medicine, we must conduct rigorous long-term evaluations under careful conditions to uncover unintended consequences or undesirable side-effects of programs that we create based on any theory. This need is especially true when the programs are different from historically accepted approaches. Short-term research is not sufficient.

The High/Scope Preschool Curriculum study raises important questions about preschool curriculum approaches for professionals and policymakers concerned with equity and the amelioration of social problems. While not the definitive study by any means, the critical issues it raises regarding the proper education of our children beg for further discussion.

EDITOR'S NOTE: The findings of the High/Scope study, comparing the three programs, remain controversial. Carl Bereiter, of the Centre for Applied Cognitive Science at The Ontario Institute for Studies in Education, who is a pioneer of "direct instruction"— the teacher-directed version of the three programs—challenges High/Scope's research methods and findings, questioning its reliance on self-reported delinquencies and the unequal number of males and females in the sample, among other issues. In addition, he denies that his program's management is based on Skinnerian behaviorism.

High/Scope spokesmen, standing by what they consider the integrity of their research, point out that they emphasized that the small sample of their study makes its findings by no means definitive. They urge further research.

While early childhood experts will continue to debate these issues, the data thus far presented, though by no means final, will help parents and professionals in their search for the right kind of program for different purposes and different children. F.M.H.

CHAPTER FOUR

A TALE OF THREE CHILDREN IN THREE PRESCHOOLS

by Nancy Curry

Even prior to Head Start, most of us in early childhood education were committed to high-quality education. We taught the relatively small number of adults in training and we provided education for a relatively small number of children. In the past twenty years the whirlwind of activities and the astonishingly rapid expansion of our field have thrust our profession into the limelight. What we knew about quality was challenged by colleagues from related fields, and we worked hard to explicate what had been implicit or, we thought, self-explanatory.

The tremendous pressures to meet the personnel needs of the mushrooming Head Start programs and day-care centers resulted often in less-than-optimal quality, and we had the uneasy feeling that we were doing the best we could, but it did not seem good enough.

Now private providers and proprietary centers are rushing in to fill the gap in services resulting from cutbacks in feder-

This account of three children in different day-care settings suggests that curriculum is not the only variable that affects school quality. The teacher's manner, style, and philosophy have a critical effect. Nancy Curry is director of the Program in Child Development and Child Care at the University of Pittsburgh. This report was originally published in 1985 by the High/Scope Educational Research Foundation.

ally funded programs and from the large number of women entering or returning to the work force and requiring care for their children. We are again painfully aware of the lack of good quality care.

Early childhood programs no longer deal only with children aged three to eight. They now include infant and toddler centers; nursery schools; day-care centers and family day-care homes for children from birth to school age; and, of course, private and public kindergartens. I am working on the assumption that all children are being educated, in any program they attend, and therefore should be included in a discussion of early childhood education. Whether they are learning what we want them to learn we cannot be sure, but we *can* be sure that they are adapting to the conditions provided for their care and in that sense are learning for better or worse.

IS QUALITY JUST TRIAL AND ERROR?

I challenge the premise that the common-sense approach to early childhood seems to be working. Our field has been extremely vulnerable to the idea that anyone can work with children—after all, we all were children, or we have had children, or we know well our neighborhood and relatives' children. We all live in some kind of a building, we may even own our own homes, but this intimate acquaintanceship common to all of us does not qualify us to be architects. My point is that education of young children calls for highly trained professionals who have not only an aptitude for, but also a commitment to, educating themselves as well as the children whom they teach. We can indeed codify or measure good early childhood practices, and these spring not only from common sense but also from a solid theoretical base with supervised practical experiences. We should no longer view ourselves as a paraprofessional field aimed at providing jobs for adults (the poor, the aged) but should recognize that we have come of age as a profession with all these hallmarks of a profession:

—A research-based body of knowledge
—Professional journals to disseminate knowledge
—Professional organizations to share experience and knowledge
—Readily available professional education at the college and university level
—Career ladders within the profession

Secondly, we do not need to rediscover by trial and error what works with children. We have our developmental and educational theorists to generate research in tandem with the practitioners, who often know what works but also want to know what works best. And we now have the research that shows what contributes to quality and what can happen when poor quality prevails in early childhood programs. Our systematic observations as practitioners can continue to spark the research that will guide the practices so necessary to improve quality in early childhood education.

THREE EVERYDAY EXAMPLES

Eighteen-month-old Joey attends a local learning center from 7:00 A.M. to 6:00 P.M. daily. He arrives at the center with donut crumbs on his face and is yawning and often tearful on saying goodbye to his mother or father, especially now that the summer staff has been replaced by a new group of teachers. His brother attends the same center but is in a different class, since the children are segregated by age.

The teacher notes that Joey is usually quiet, even withdrawn, except for the occasional times when he spies his brother in the hall and runs to embrace him or when he cuddles up to a new young teacher to whom he seems to be attached and to whom he clings if permitted. Joey pays little attention to his peers, except for an occasional bout of biting, for which he is disciplined by being put in the "time out" highchair. This doesn't seem to stop him, says his teacher, for he usually falls asleep in that chair. "Time out is no use."

Except for his biting forays, Joey is docile, demands little attention, and "seems lost in the crowd." He only cries hard when one of his parents arrives to pick him up. His tears are greeted with exasperation and no little puzzlement by his exhausted parents, who face an evening with two tired, hungry little boys.

Joey's mother hasn't had time to tell the teacher that he has been waking nightly for several weeks, screaming and shaking with terror and begging to be taken into his parents' bed, a demand they sometimes accede to in order to get a decent night's sleep.

Four-year-old Cathy spends her extended day at a local day-care center. When she arrives at 7:30 A.M., the male teacher (her favorite) greets her with a free lap and a mutual conversation about the toy koala bear she carries. Cathy's best friend, April, age 3½, whom she has played with in the neighborhood for a year, arrives at 8:00 A.M., and the two girls exchange hugs and gravitate toward the housekeeping corner, where they engage in an ongoing game of mother/baby horse, alternating roles.

Cathy chooses the breakfast table of her favorite teacher (who was her teacher last year, as well). He and the children discuss yesterday's trip to the local bakery. While she protests mildly at the morning rest period and loudly at the afternoon nap time, Cathy settles down both times with thumb in mouth and with her other hand on the knee of her teacher, seated nearby. She participates freely during free time in long bouts of dramatic play; paints several easel pictures to take home; pouts at story time when she can't pick the daily story; then recuperates in time to join the dancing, flushing with triumph at getting one of the boys to be her partner.

Outdoors Cathy is active and works out a spat with April over who is to ride the favorite red school tricycle. She ends her day by competently completing several wooden puzzles and playing several rounds of *Candyland* with her teacher and April.

When her father picks her up at 5:00 P.M., she is heavy-lidded and somewhat whiny, but eager to show him a painting her teacher has placed at her eye-level, right inside the front door. Her parents report that she chatters endlessly about "my school" and "my Mr. Anderson."

Three-year-old Matt attends a long-established neighborhood nursery in a predominantly working-class neighborhood. The nursery has recently been placed under new sponsorship, and the new director is eager to make her mark as an efficient administrator who "runs a tight ship." The center is bright, clean, and orderly, with adult art covering the bulletin boards, which are placed at adult eye-level. The children are orderly, quiet, and even a little subdued, with the explicit understanding that there is to be no fighting either with each other or indirectly with miniature-life toys, and no running within the building.

There is a place for every toy, and toys are to be used in specified ways; for example, puzzles and manipulative toys are to be used only at the table nearest the shelves where the toys are kept.

A visitor to Matt's center notices the quiet in the building when she drops by at 10:30 A.M. to supervise a college student. The silence is broken by a faint wail that grows louder as a small three-year-old and her shamefaced mother leave the classroom with an admonishing farewell from the teacher, "Perhaps you can stay longer tomorrow, Sally, if you don't cry."

The visitor is greeted by the center director, who ushers her into the classroom with a proud comment that the children are so orderly and well behaved. The visitor notes that Matt is sitting in a corner, aimlessly running a little car back and forth over a block. Another little boy places his car on the block and the two vehicles collide. Matt's face brightens, he runs his car into the other child's, and both boys give a shout of delight. The teacher stiffens, the room grows more silent, and the other children watch with wide eyes as she moves to the block area and says kindly but firmly, "Matt, you know the rule. No hitting with cars." Matt slumps back to his former position and begins to run the car back and forth again over the block. The director smiles approvingly at the teacher and the boys, and one little girl says softly to her friend, "Matt's a bad boy!"

After an hour's observation, the visitor is struck with the number of children who claim to be cold and wrap the student teacher's arms around their shivering bodies; to her the room seems rather warm. She realizes that this is the only time the children have any close contact with any member of the teaching staff.

I have deliberately drawn examples from early childhood centers that by some standards would be considered good, rather than citing the hair-raising examples we are all familiar with—children in custodial care with little space, punitive adults, broken equipment, slipshod housekeeping, programs that stress academics for babies, and so on. Such conditions are readily detectable, and should be shut down. What is more difficult is to recognize the more subtle good versus poor points. I suggest that we look at the children in these programs and see how the quality affects their development.

What is impressive in looking at the three centers is the adaptability of the youngsters.

Eighteen-month-old Joey has adapted to his "learning center," which he attends for fifty-five hours of the week—longer than either of his parents spends on the job. But at what price?

Three-year-old Matt is indeed the compliant, subdued little boy his nursery school expects the children to be, but again, at what price? Are we cognizant of a child's critical periods in emotional development? Look at the emotional toll of an eighteen-month-old who is becoming withdrawn, passive, and apathetic in the face of what may be intolerable demands, such as being away from home for eleven out of the twenty-four hours of his day, with well-meaning but ever-changing caregivers.

With these clinical examples as a background, let us turn to what we as practitioners know constitutes high-quality early childhood education. If we consider Joey, the eighteen-month-old, or Cathy, the lively, self-directed four-year-old, we note what personality characteristics distinguish each child, what flags concern for Joey and pleasure in Cathy.

High-quality education makes it possible for Cathy to be self-directed; to be in tune with her own feelings and those of others, with a wide range of emotions; to be securely attached to parents and teachers; yet to be appropriately independent, with a lively curiosity, an eagerness to learn, and ability to use her ideas creatively. These are qualities we want to see in our children. While we cannot give all the credit to her preschool experience, we can see how her teachers facilitate her development.

By the same token, we can tell to a certain extent what is missing from Joey's life at his center—what is undermining his personality at a crucial point in his development.

Similarly, we see how Matt's center actively cultivates personality traits that please his teacher and perhaps his parents, but worry those of us who understand child development.

QUALITY AND THE PRACTITIONER

There can be no doubt about the impact of adults on very young children. The quality of the adults is the single most important aspect of an early childhood program. It is the teacher/caregiver whose philosophy determines the environment and the curriculum. It is the teacher who decides how much contact she or he will have with parents and who sets the tone for the children's everyday life. Children, as the most developed offspring of living species, have the longest period of childhood during which they are dependent on adults for nurturance, support, learning, and survival itself. We know the importance of the parent/infant bond from the beginning of life, and we are learning more and more about the importance of a strong parent/child attachment. This attachment insures the gradually unfolding separation-individuation process, which results in the child's achieving, during the first three years of life, a lasting sense of self-constancy and an abiding sense of the constancy of others.

Consider the example of Joey, the eighteen-month-old, who is at the developmentally appropriate phase to be struggling with issues of psychic separation and autonomy. At this time in his development, two essential symbol systems are emerging—speech and symbolic play. For these symbolic functions, the child needs the nourishment that comes from the consistent contact of a caring, meaningful adult.

Joey's teachers are caring people, but they shift and change, with no single adult invested in his development to the same extent as his parents, who care very much, but have little energy left at the end of the day to engage in the meaningful interchanges necessary to foster optimal symbolic growth. Because of his growing cognitive capacities and self-awareness, Joey is especially vulnerable to separation. He needs adults to help him through the daily rough spots—the transition from home to school, from lunchtime to nap, from one school play activity to another, and back home again. At this stage, a knowledgeable teacher could foster Joey's growth toward autonomy and a firm sense of self, but the center's unstable staffing prevents this, with resultant danger signs of apathy, withdrawal, and passivity.

We know the value of adults for modeling playfulness, task concentration and completion, expressions and handling of feelings, modes of relating to others, and the myriad other aspects of adults with which children identify. Matt has learned at age three that good boys do not shout, are not aggressive, are clean and neat, and do not cry when mother leaves. The sense of badness that gets engendered when he either acts out or merely feels these normal aggressive impulses is exacerbated by his knowledge that his beloved teacher will not approve.

Both Matt and Joey are showing signs of maladaptive behavior in their very adaptation to poor-quality teaching that ignores their developmental needs. Teachers must recognize and work with children's feelings. The normal feelings of childhood—love, hate, jealousy, fear, pleasure, anger, willfulness, for example—must be respected by caring adults, and their expression must be accepted and absorbed by the adult when the child cannot handle the intensity of these feelings.

Joey's biting is only one symptom of his inability to handle feelings of loss, fear, rage, and despair around separation; being placed in the "time out" chair leaves him alone and overwhelmed. He retreats into sleep.

Matt's aggressive impulses get nipped in the bud by the teacher, and he retreats into empty play, feeling ashamed and quietly angry. The caring adult transmits his or her confidence that the children eventually will be able to express and control their feelings in ways acceptable to themselves and to others (adults and other children) who mean so much to them. In the meantime, the adult serves as the model showing that feelings are important and that there are ways to manage them.

Turning now to Cathy's good-quality day-care center, we learn that her teachers are well-trained in a child development program that intertwines theory, research, practice, and programming. The teachers know the importance of finely honed empathy. Inservice education allows them to refuel when their teaching grows stale, and good supervision enables them to sort out their ideas and feelings with another understanding and knowledgeable adult whenever they find themselves too close to a problem to deal with it objectively.

In Cathy's classroom, she is valued as an individual with needs, interests, and capacities, which the teachers foster through an individualized program built on their knowledge of her developmental readiness. They recognize and channel the children's feelings, to provide direct and indirect learning experiences, to facilitate play, to foster autonomy but provide nurturance and meet needs for dependence when appropriate.

Above all, these teachers see their roles as supplementary to the home. They make sure Cathy's parents know what happened during her school day; they take time to hear her parents' concerns. They encourage relationships between children: a good teacher knows how much teaching goes on between children—how one child, amazed at the different style and daring of another child, models him/herself after the other. Through their shared puzzlement, shared experiences, and shared views of a newly emerging, mystifying world, children can understand, and communicate with, each other at levels of empathy beyond the adult's reach. But it takes an aware adult to mediate, facilitate, guide, and occasionally ignore this learning between children, in order for it to take shape in constructive, expanding ways.

QUALITY AND THE ENVIRONMENT

A school's physical environment tells a great deal about its philosophy. On entering an early childhood center, we are immediately aware of how adults value the children and themselves. It is easy to detect a poor environment—broken toys, a haphazard arrangement of equipment, dirty sinks and smelly toilets, unkempt shelves and lockers, torn books, and a general air of neglect and carelessness. There are important, sometimes subtle, differences in centers that affect children. The environment sends a message to adults and children alike.

Matt's center, which is pleasant and welcoming to the adult, is maintained with an eye to order and cleanliness, both laudable standards. However, when these standards dominate all aspects of children's behaviors, then we know that the teachers are putting their adult needs for control and order ahead of the child's need to experiment, to try out various ways of using materials, to occasionally glory in play with fluid and plastic materials (in spite of their messiness), and to have a sense that this is their school as well as the teachers'. The placement of toys and pictures tells a great deal about whom the rooms are for; pictures at the eye-level of adults are pleasing to adults but cannot be enjoyed by children. The selection of adult rather than children's art tells us whose products are valued most.

We know that overcrowded, messy classrooms with too many children and too few adults lead to disorganized messy play and aimless rushing about. Well-planned environments with an adequate adult/child ratio are conducive to constructive learning, including rich dramatic play episodes. In his review of services for children under age five in Britain, specifically in Oxfordshire, Jerome Bruner concludes that smaller, well-staffed centers encourage conversation and promote dramatic play better than do larger, more sparsely staffed centers.

In sum, the environment of a high-quality center reflects the philosophy of the teachers, since they make the decisions about room arrangements, selection of materials, and programming. A program of quality has rooms arranged for the children's convenience, visibility, and accessibility. Areas are well defined, so that ongoing play does not get disrupted and children can easily pursue their individual and group interests. Materials are selected to appeal to specific ages and to lend themselves to the symbolization of the children's experience. Knowledge of the varying developmental needs of children leads us to supply duplicate toys for younger children who cannot yet share and postpone, unstructured toys that will give scope to imagination and improvisation, structured toys that are self-correcting and lead to a sense of efficacy, and, above all, the teacher's permission and encouragement for the creative uses of the materials in a multiplicity of ways.

QUALITY AND ESPOUSING A THEORY

High-quality early childhood programs must espouse a philosophy—a set of guiding principles for the education of young children based in theory and research. Our profession has come of age through the careful, thoughtful implementation of various philosophical positions based on various theories—maturation, behavioral/environmental, and cognitive/developmental. Each of these theoretical positions as implemented in experimental programs has had some payoff for the children. Whether or not we totally agree with a program's philosophy, there is comfort in knowing that the teachers have made a commitment to a philosophy and have a rationale for what they do that is backed by research and tested practice.

In the examples cited earlier, Joey's center does not appear to be operating under theoretically based guiding principles, other than those involving the health, safety, and perhaps nutrition of the children. The staff are well-meaning, operate on a day-to-day basis, have little investment in furthering their knowledge, and see their primary purpose as providing safe day care for profit under the label of a "learning center."

Matt's center has a philosophy with no apparent theoretical base. The guiding principle seems to be that of adult control and child obedience, and the staff works assiduously toward that goal. This pays off for them and reinforces their philosophy, for they are getting the kind of behavior they want from the children; their center is quiet and orderly.

Other centers are going "back to basics," introducing letters and numbers earlier and earlier to very young children. This theoretical stance has no solid base or research to show what ultimate payoff it has for children.

Cathy's day care center implements a sound philosophy. The school's environment encourages each child to be an active partner in the learning process—the actor, the doer, the initiator. The curriculum is determined by the children, each of whom is seen as an individual with a unique endowment that has been, and continues to be, influenced by the child's social and cultural environment. The adult does not abdicate his or her responsibility for building on the children's ideas and for providing the nutriment for further learning that challenges the children to reach out for new experiences. In Cathy's school, children's needs, interests, and developmental capacities determine the program content, the room arrangement, and the way the daily activities are devised. The teachers know the importance of pacing: children are challenged by enough novelty to be intrigued but not by so much that they tune out. The teachers see themselves as facilitators and are readily available to help the children succeed. They do not dominate the activities or the children, and they consider that classroom and activities belong to both the children and the teachers.

For example, Cathy's interest in horses is acknowledged by her teachers and encouraged by the introduction of pictures, puzzles, books, and an occasional song. When she builds a corral with blocks, they respect her wish to keep it up overnight for a continuation of her horse play the next day;

but they do not develop a unit on horses for the entire class, since this appears to be Cathy's unique interest.

Such a philosophy cannot be implemented solely through teachers' common sense and intuition. Teachers need a thorough grounding in the following:

1. The principles governing growth and development of all human beings—such as the gestalt notions of the progression from global diffuseness, to differentiation, to organization and integration; Margaret Mahler's theories of separation and individuation; Jean Piaget's concepts of assimilation and accommodation; and Erik Erikson's psychosocial changes

2. The slow and continuing accumulation of knowledge and disputation concerning the best ways of educating the young child—which has its roots in the philosophies of John Locke, Jean Henri Pestalozzi, J. J. Rousseau, Frederich Froebel, John Dewey, and Maria Montessori

3. The factors in the short life-history of the child that influence his present behavior (what children have in common; and how and why they differ from each other)

This philosophical approach calls for acceptance of the child's intense urge to play. Play serves an essential function in furthering the child's developing symbolic functions. As the child moves from the sensorimotor period to the preoperational mode of thought characteristic of the later preschool years, an elaborate system of symbolization develops in the second year of life. Both receptive and expressive language capacities grow, so that the child can indicate needs, wishes, and feelings symbolically, rather than having to act them out directly. Differentiation of self from others is made possible by language—the child creates the words; sees that other people, objects, and things have labels; and can use these labels in a common symbolic system. Using this common system makes the child a part of the world at the same time the child is finding that he or she exists separately in that world.

We are seriously concerned about Joey, who lacks the opportunity to realize this potential. His signals are not being heard. Consequently, he may be stunted in his development of the capacity to symbolize, which assists the child in becoming autonomous, efficient in learning, and effective in the environment.

One expects a three-year-old to begin to use dramatic play as an integrative function in the symbolic process. In rudimentary dramatic play, the child depicts what has been observed or experienced and, in the process, symbolizes both external and internal reality. To be able to play-act an event (pretending one drives home from work, like mommy) or to replicate in play a real emotion (pretending to be sad) is a further step in abstraction. Matt, through the inhibition of his normal aggressive drive, does not seem to have the energy to engage in the zestful play most three-year-olds enjoy. In his efforts to control himself and be the docile child his teacher values, he does not use play to learn about his world and his place in it. His desultory attempts at play tell us instead how he feels about himself in his world—helpless and ineffectual.

Cathy, on the other hand, uses play meaningfully and is furthering her social, emotional, physical, and intellectual growth through play. Her dramatic play has a discernible beginning, middle, and end, and she has the ability to sustain her roles as mother/baby/daddy/horse even when she gets distracted. Her interest in horses leads her to seek out the available stimuli about these animals, and at age four she is a walking encyclopedia about the various breeds of horses, just as her classmate Jim knows all about dinosaurs. Her capacity to keep her younger friend April involved in the extended horse-episodes tells us of her ability to see things from another's point of view, for she will adapt, shift, and accommodate to April's wishes for the sake of sustaining play. Further, she has captured the essence of the horse's movements, for she can canter down the halls in an uncanny imitation of a real horse. From her play capacities, she demonstrates conservation, reversibility, problem solving, and creativity, and playfulness—all attributes essential to learning.

The emotional investment in such play tells us of its importance to this little girl, and her teachers understand it in the context of what they know of her family life and what she is struggling with. Since she swings flexibly between the nurturing and aggressive aspects in her portrayal of the role, can maintain a distinction between real and pretend, and has a flexible array of other self-representations, teachers feel comfortable in facilitating her play by providing time, space, materials, and their approval of her and her playmates' role-playing abilities.

Such an appreciation of children's play could make the difference for Joey and Matt in their school setting, but it does not happen; they are cut off from a self-expressive avenue that could aid in their adjustments to both home and school realities. Our concern is, of course, for their emotional development; but without the opportunity to symbolize, integrate, and synthesize their internal and external realities, their intellectual growth is becoming stunted as well.

The quality of our children's education can make a difference in their lives. We have the means and responsibility to define and implement high quality in early childhood education. The theoretical orientation of the centers, the curriculum, and the environment all play a strong part in the assurance of high quality; but it is the people, young and old, who really make the difference. Children deserve the best teachers we can provide—teachers well trained in child development and early childhood methodologies and with a capacity for nurture, empathy, and deep respect for the developing human beings in their care.

CHAPTER FIVE

A SCHOOL-BASED PROGRAM FROM INFANCY TO KINDERGARTEN FOR CHILDREN AND THEIR PARENTS

by Donald E. Pierson, Deborah Klein Walker, and Terrence Tivnan

In November 1972 the Public Schools of Brookline, Massachusetts began a long-term demonstration and research effort entitled the Brookline Early Education Project (BEEP). The program has sought answers to these questions: Should public schools consider offering early education programs? What are the essential components of an effective early education program? Is it feasible for a public school to sustain an effective early education program?

In the planning stages for several years prior to 1972, the project has attempted to incorporate the best advice of local school personnel and community representatives and nation-

Are the activities within a school/center program enough for preschoolers? To what extent must effective preschool programs reach out to parents? These questions are explored in this report of the Brookline (Massachusetts) Early Education Project. This article originally appeared in The Personnel and Guidance Journal.

ally prominent experts in education, psychology, health care, research design, and social policy. Over the past eleven years, Carnegie Corporation of New York and The Robert Wood Johnson Foundation have subsidized the project's planning, the delivery of pilot services, and the current evaluation work. The superintendent of schools has consistently designated early education as a top priority, helping to gain the interest and cooperation of the staff and community.

Three categories of related programs and previous research are pertinent to considerations for the school's role in early education.

It is widely acknowledged that despite changing family structures and regardless of child-care arrangements, parents are the most influential teachers of their young children. It therefore seems that if schools were to form alliances with parents during the children's earliest years, child and family strengths could be recognized and potential weaknesses could be addressed, minimizing the exacerbation of serious educational problems. Parents and teachers could learn to communicate with each other before the tensions of academic concerns surfaced.

A rapidly growing number and variety of agencies offer support to families of young children. This grass roots movement is a response to the isolation and stress experienced by families in the U.S. today. The groups include prenatal couples, adolescent mothers, working mothers, fathers, nursing mothers, parents of twins, and many others with some common interest. The underlying theme for these groups is "helping families to help themselves." With limited funds for research and evaluation, few systematic assessments have been made of the effects of these programs on children and parents. Parents and staff testify with anecdotal evidence that dramatic impacts often occur on parental coping abilities.

School systems invest a great deal more in the education of adolescents than in elementary-age children, most public schools invest negligible amounts in the education of children younger than six years of age. The National Commission on Educational Excellence has recommended more of the same medicine for the current educational malaise, for example, longer school days and longer academic years. This reflects a circumstance in which educators, health-care professionals, public policymakers, and too many parents ignore the potential for learning (by children and by parents) in the early childhood years.

Most of our research knowledge about the effects of early education has come from studies of center-based preschool programs for children from low-income families. Measures of short-term program impact have traditionally focused on gains rather than on school competence or other indices consistent with the major program goals.

All families residing in Brookline were invited to enroll in BEEP if they had a child born during the enrollment period, from spring 1973 to fall 1974. To gain more diversity than would be possible in Brookline alone and to maintain a consistency with Brookline's efforts toward urban-suburban desegregation, ethnic minority families in adjoining areas of Boston were also eligible to join. To minimize the self-selection process that might result in an excess of education-oriented parents, outreach strategies were employed to recruit families who ordinarily would not hear about or seek out such an innovative program. School counselors and social workers, town health and welfare departments, local obstetricians, and neighborhood contacts were all helpful in the recruiting.

When enrollment closed in October 1974, 285 families had signed up. These constituted the pilot group with whom the project worked until the children entered kindergarten at five years of age. The pilot group reflected the diversity and background characteristics that were sought in the recruiting campaign. For example, 39 percent were ethnic minority families, 50 percent of the mothers had less than a college education, 18 percent did not speak English as a first language in the home, and 12 percent were single-parent families. The ages of the mothers at enrollment ranged from fourteen to forty-one years.

The focal point for most project activities was the BEEP Center, a former college dormitory located near the Brookline-Boston boundary. The Center housed the research and administration offices and many of the programs for children and parents. With a lending library of books and toys, meeting rooms, and indoor and outdoor play areas for children, the Center served as a convenient place where families could drop in informally whenever they liked. As the children turned three, space became available in several of the Brookline elementary schools to house the prekindergarten classes.

BEEP programs consisted of three interrelated components based on the preceding rationale.

1. Parent Education and Support. Committed to the idea that the family is the most important educational force for the young child, BEEP worked to inform and support parents by providing valid information and nurturant resources. Teaching staff, selected to reflect the cultural and ethnic backgrounds of the families, were expected to be both experts trained in child development and friends who were parents themselves and who realized there were no simple answers to the challenge of child rearing.

The amount of parent education offered to each family was controlled by random assignment of families to one of three levels of program intensity. The most expensive level (projected at $1,200* per child per year) involved frequent home visits, meetings, and limited child care during meetings, each scheduled at least once every four weeks. The second or moderate level of program intensity ($800) involved the same offerings less frequently, with appointments scheduled about once every six weeks. The least expensive cost level ($400) involved no outreach through home visits, meetings, or child care. Information and support were available at BEEP and by telephone, but parents had to exert initiative to take advantage of the opportunities. Transportation to the Center, a lending library of books and toys, and the "BEEP News" newsletter were available to all families.

As the children became involved in programs of their own from twenty-four months on, the more expensive home visits

---

*Note: Amounts represent 1972 dollars.

were largely supplanted by modes of parent-staff interaction that focused on the child's behavior in school (e.g., parent-teacher conferences and guided observations of the classroom). Discussions between parents and staff centered around recognizing the child's strengths and needs and sharing expectations for the child. Teachers participated in weekly inservice training and were closely supervised to ensure that curriculum guidelines were implemented.

2. Diagnostic Monitoring. All children enrolled in BEEP received periodic health and developmental exams to ensure that no child would progress through the preschool years with some undetected health or developmental condition that might hamper abilities to function successfully in school. The exams were held at very frequent intervals: two weeks, three months, six months, fourteen months, twenty-four months, thirty months, forty-two months, and entry into kindergarten. This frequency was primarily for research purposes, and it was assumed that any future partial replications of BEEP would be able to reduce the number of exams.

Through collaboration with Children's Hospital Medical Center, a multidisciplinary team conducted the physical, neurologic, and developmental assessments at the BEEP Center. Parents were expected to observe the exams, and results were shared verbally and in writing. A copy of each written report was sent, with parent permission, to the primary-care physician.

3. Education Programs for Children. Beginning at age two, weekly playgroups were held for small groups of six to eight children. Each session followed a predictable routine (e.g., planning time, art, story telling, rhythm activity, snack, and discussion) that was geared to the developmental levels of the children. Parents were expected to observe the sessions frequently and to discuss mutual insights with the teaching staff.

At ages three and four, BEEP participants had the option of a daily morning prekindergarten program. Classes typically consisted of fifteen to twenty children and three adults. Several classes were bilingual. Curriculum emphasis, influenced by the High/Scope Program, was on structuring the space and materials to afford each child an opportunity to develop a sense of effectiveness, to explore concepts, and to develop mastery and social skills essential for competencies in school. Individual goals for the child, parents, and teacher were mutually determined by teachers and parents. Teachers compiled daily written plans and extensive records on the children's daily progress. An interdisciplinary diagnostic team was available to advise appropriate action for children whose needs required special attention.

The prekindergarten program was the only phase of BEEP in which parents were asked to share the program expense. A sliding scale fee was established that ranged from $25 to $800 per child per year, based on each family's expressed ability to pay. Extended day care was available each afternoon in the same setting.

THE RESULTS

The assesement of a comprehensive, longitudinal education program is both difficult and important. BEEP's approach to evaluating the program's effectiveness was to use a variety of techniques and perspectives (e.g., teacher, parent, independent observer, etc.) rather than relying on any single test or measure of effectiveness. Thus, the evaluation effort considered the impact on parents and on children's performance in several areas of school competence. Similarly, it was important to be able to measure impact of the program at several points in time (e.g., age thirty months, entry to kindergarten, second grade), looking for both short-term and long-term outcomes.

The results presented here are drawn from assessments of children made during the spring of second grade, three years after the termination of BEEP services. Earlier results of the evaluation at kindergarten indicated significant advantages for BEEP children in several areas of social behavior and other kindergarten skills as documented by independent observations. Ratings obtained from kindergarten teachers indicated that BEEP was particularly effective for subgroups of children who might ordinarily be expected to have more difficulties in adjusting to school.

The evaluation measures in the second grade were generally similar to those used in kindergarten. Classroom learning behaviors were assessed by observing children individually within their classrooms. Independent observers, who were not informed about the program participation of any of the children, carried out a series of six ten-minute observations on each BEEP child and other children who were selected at random from the same classroom as the BEEP participants.

Other assessments of children's performance were obtained from the second-grade classroom teachers. In particular, teachers were asked to report the reading level of each child by providing information on the book and basal reading series in which each child was able to read and comprehend stories during the spring of second grade.

Several family background characteristics, such as parents' education and proportions of single-parent families, were quite similar for BEEP participants and the comparison children. BEEP had a slightly higher proportion of Spanish-speaking families; the comparison group had a slightly higher proportion of families with other first languages (e.g., Chinese, Russian, and Hebrew).

The results obtained from the observations of children's classroom learning behaviors show that the children's rate of difficulty for BEEP participants (14.2 percent) was only one-half that found for the randomly selected comparison group (28.4 percent). The behaviors observed included skills such as working independently, following directions, resisting distractions, completing work successfully, getting along with other children, and involvement in classroom activities. This overall advantage for BEEP participants was quite consistent regardless of the background characteristics of the children. That is, the advantage for BEEP participants was found both among children with well-educated parents and among children whose parents were less well-educated. The advantages were present for boys as well as for girls.

The percentages of children who were unable to decode or

comprehend stories in a 2-2 level basal reader during the spring of second grade shows a statistically significant difference favoring BEEP participants: 19.3 percent of BEEP children were not performing up to this standard, as compared to 32.5 percent of the comparison children.

As a further investigation of the effectiveness of BEEP, analyses were carried out to determine whether the level of program intensity the parents experienced would show any effect on the children's later performance. An additional aspect of this question was whether the type of program that would be most effective might depend on some characteristics of the participating families. Is a more intensive and expensive parent outreach program necessary and more effective for all families, or are some types of families more likely than others to benefit from a particular level of services?

School-based early education can make a difference in elementary school performance for diverse groups of children. The measurable benefits in reading and classroom learning behaviors were not restricted to children whose parents were either highly educated or of limited educational background. For the children whose parents lacked a higher education, the program was effective only when sufficient parent-staff contacts were expected and scheduled. An impact on parents was manifested in the pattern of parent-teacher contacts at second grade.

The overall results favoring BEEP participants in second grade are similar to the results obtained in kindergarten. But the second grade findings extend our knowledge in important ways. In the kindergarten evaluation the major overall effects were found in the area of children's social skills and interactions. This was not surprising given the nature of the kindergarten classrooms. The results at second grade provide evidence that children's academic performance was also influenced. Thus, the impact on social skills observed in kindergarten may have extended to areas of mastery skills and reading level at grade two. It is important to note that these results indicate fewer children were having problems in school, not that BEEP services had raised the overall level of performance or produced children performing far above grade level. This reduction of school-related difficulties is in accord with the project's primary goal.

BEEP's demonstrated success in preventing difficulties in school involved interrelated components of parent education and support, periodic health and developmental monitoring, and early childhood programs. Although it is likely that not all of these components were equally important in helping all families, it is not possible at this stage of our research knowledge to isolate the impact of any single component. BEEP services were provided as a comprehensive package to families and, rather than imposing a rigid schedule of service delivery, the services were individualized as much as possible to meet the needs of the diverse group of families enrolled. It is important that future programs design partial replications, reducing and adapting the services they offer to suit other settings and other groups of families. The theoretical thrust of BEEP and the evidence of impact on parent-teacher communication patterns suggest that foremost attention be given to the parent education and support function. Thus, the results from BEEP are in accord with other evidence on the key role of parent involvement in effective early education programs.

The cost-effectiveness analyses underscore that schools must reach out more to families with limited educational backgrounds. If an impact on school competence is desired, it is not enough just to establish a drop-in center for these families. The investment must be substantial, closer to $2,000 than $1,000 per child per year in 1984 dollars. Though early education for low-income families must not be presented as a panacea for inadequate food, housing, and other life necessities, our results suggest corroboration for the Weber, Foster, and Weikart analyses. That is, if the proportion of children that attain competency standards can be increased from about 50 percent to more than 70 percent, then the returns on the investment will far outweigh the cost. Surely, if equality of educational opportunity is to be realized, the efforts must start before five years of age.

On the other hand, for highly educated families some coordination but less public investment is warranted. These families have adequate resources and are able to exercise much initiative. If information and support are made available about topics such as normal child development, behavior, management, and criteria for choosing high-quality child care, highly educated families will find their own way. With inexpensive but systematic attention, the unnecessary failures in elementary school for children whose families have economic and educational advantages can practically be eliminated.

BEEP is a primary prevention effort that encompasses the interrelated fields of public education, maternal and child health, mental health, and social services. The multidisciplinary orientation demonstrated in Brookline involves a public school taking the lead in assuring (but not necessarily providing) resources for parent information and support, adequate health care, developmental assessments, optimum early child stimulation, case coordination, and advocacy. In the event that schools in certain areas are unable or unwilling to take this leadership role, the challenge is left to other community agencies. Realistically, financial incentives from state agencies or private corporations and foundations will often be necessary to achieve local impetus. But because the benefits are obvious, families with adequate incomes can also be expected to pay for a portion of these educational programs.

The BEEP model has demonstrated, not that teachers and parents should work in isolation, but that two or three "heads" are better than one in planning and conducting early education. The individuals working together may be teacher and parents; mother and father; mother and friends; counselor and nurse; teacher, doctor, and social worker; or some other combination. In any case, the essence of this early education model is that cooperation, communication, and informal advocacy on behalf of young children can enhance prospects for improved quality of life for children.

The time has come for schools and health-care providers to act on information that is now available to them. New standards should be drawn for competent schools, for adequate pediatric care, and for effective mental health agencies. The standards give attention to collaborative programs that can prevent learning and adjustment difficulties.

CHAPTER SIX

BASICS FOR PRESCHOOLERS: The High/Scope Approach

by David P. Weikart

When the active school requires that a student's efforts come from the student himself instead of being imposed, and that his intelligence undertake authentic work instead of accepting predigested knowledge from outside, it is simply asking that the laws of all intelligence be respected.

—Jean Piaget

The High/Scope Curriculum is widely recognized as a successful approach to early childhood education. We've been around for a long time. Perhaps that's why I'm being asked more and more often to identify how our curriculum approach has changed to meet the changing times.

Yes, we have changed some things, and we are always open to new ideas that will enhance young children's learning. But the core of our approach remains the same. We have come to realize, more than ever, just how important it is to approach children *where they are,* not *where we want them to be.*

Many principles of early education are still evolving. Professionals, nevertheless increasingly agree that the child must have a direct role in choosing the course and pace of his or her learning. This article, published in the spring 1986 issue of High/Scope ReSource *(High/Scope Press), describes the way the High/Scope program has put this philosophy into practice.*

I have written this article not as a defense but as a challenge. I challenge all early childhood educators, policymakers, and parents to stem the tide: to resist the increasing pressures to teach young children facts and figures before they are ready, and to focus instead on nurturing their special skills and abilities.

The view of what children's learning should be, as set forth by Swiss psychologist Jean Piaget, is summed up in the quotation that leads this article. We adopted this view as we began our curriculum development efforts more than twenty years ago; we continue to believe in it today.

PRESCHOOLERS' SPECIAL VIEW OF THE WORLD

"Mommy, you'd better hurry! The moon's following us and may eat the car." The four-year-old who made this statement is not trying to be "cute"; she is making a reasonable attempt to explain something in her world. Her thinking is typical of children in what Piaget called the *preoperational* stage of development.

One of Piaget's revolutionary ideas was that children's thinking is not an incomplete version of adult thinking, but rather a *qualitatively different process*. The things children say that make adults laugh or scratch their heads are not meant to be entertaining. Nor can adults talk children out of these thought patterns. *Only through many direct experiences that challenge their thinking and employ their emerging skills will children abandon their preoperational logic and move on to the next cognitive level.*

Children's thinking changes only when they have accumulated enough evidence over time to make change necessary. Adults can aid this process by pointing out inconsistencies: "If the moon wants to catch us, why does it stop chasing us when we stop the car?" But adults should not expect children to abandon their patterns of thinking just on the strength of an older person's explanation.

Adults can work with preschoolers more effectively if they

are aware of some of the special qualities of the "preoperational" child's thought processes:

Inability to conserve. Most preschoolers tend to base judgments about number and amount completely on appearances. For example, 3½-year-old Alicia says that a row of seven pennies spread out over the top of a desk contains more pennies than a row of seven pennies spread out over a notebook. She believes that since the first row is longer, it contains more pennies.

Animism. Children consider many nonliving things to be alive because they move or in some way look alive. Three-year-old Corey, for example, watching butter melt in a frying pan, cries excitedly, "It's running!" When asked if that means the butter is alive, he replies, "Yes, because it's moving."

Literalness. Preoperational children take language at its face value. When four-year-old Sally's mother scolds her for speaking inappropriately at the dinner table and tells her to "Watch your tongue," Sally sticks out her tongue and looks at it.

Blending intuitive and scientific fact. Young children sometimes explain things by using a combination of fantasy and misapplied information. For example, as Jeff is examining an apple, he notices that it is wet inside and offers the idea that the wetness in the apple comes from the rain. His friend John adds that the rain comes from Mother Nature. Jeff agrees without a minute's hesitation and demonstrates how Mother Nature makes it rain by extending his arms sideways and wiggling his fingers. In making such explanations, children are doing their best to bring their own experiences to bear on their observations. They are stretching their thinking, even if their final conclusions are not correct.

Class inclusion errors. Most preschoolers can sort things by category but cannot grasp the idea that something can belong to two categories simultaneously. For example, when Tommy is asked if his baby sister is a person, he says that she is, but when he is asked how many people there are in his family, he replies, "Three people—Mommy, Daddy, and me—and one baby!"

If we keep in mind these and similar examples as we interact with young children, our responses and encouragement will be most appropriate to their developmental level. Our role is not to correct or argue with young children's mistaken logic, or to try to force cognitive growth. Rather, it is to provide experiences that challenge children to revise their theories and, when they are ready, to develop new thinking patterns that incorporate accepted knowledge and practice.

THE "BASICS," ACCORDING TO HIGH/SCOPE

Piaget's theories guide us in our search for the best ways to support and extend preschoolers' emerging skills. True, some of his theories have been questioned, and rightly so, and other experts have come on the scene with thought-provoking suggestions and statements. We have learned, for example, that Piaget's stages of development are not as clear-cut as initially thought. Children can sometimes "think" in more mature ways than we would expect, based on Piaget's theory. Nevertheless, we believe that the "laws of intelligence," derived largely from Piaget's developmental theory and research, continue to have important implications for early childhood teaching and learning.

The fundamental premise of the High/Scope Curriculum is that children are *active learners* who learn best from activities they plan and carry out themselves.

We at High/Scope embrace the concept of "active learning" in everything we do: teacher training, research, early childhood education. In High/Scope's approach to early childhood teaching and learning, the following precepts have remained constant over our twenty-year history of research and curriculum development:

—Teachers must understand how children mentally construct the world and how these mental constructs change in the course of children's development. Teachers must assess each child's understanding of number, length, weight, space, and time, and work within each child's reasoning abilities.

—Teaching must build upon, not direct or control, the thoughts and actions of children. Since learning occurs when children become intensely involved in activities or projects of their own design, teaching means insuring that children choose and organize their own work. Teaching, then, means insuring that children's chosen work becomes a context for thinking.

—Children must have daily opportunities to decide what they want to do. The teacher helps each child develop a plan, break it into manageable pieces, define a sequence of steps, and identify needed materials. At the preschool level, the child begins to plan simply by making a commitment, which the teacher supports, to a particular activity. Over time, the child's plans will increase in range and complexity as he or she develops the ability to think about choices and decisions before acting upon them.

—The child's daily plan must provide the starting point for teaching. It's the springboard for questioning, suggesting, posing problems. The teacher helps each child think about what he or she is doing, make observations, notice relationships, and define and solve problems.

—Certain key experiences are essential to children's early intellectual growth. Guided by these key experiences, the teacher deliberately and systematically helps children predict, observe, describe, explain, manipulate, hypothesize, and find alternatives. The teacher's job is to help children incorporate these processes into their work.

These precepts have produced the unified educational theory that is described in our curriculum manual *Young Children in Action* and its accompanying *Study Guide*. They have been validated in a twenty-year longitudinal research project, as reported in the High/Scope monograph *Changed Lives: The Effects of the Perry Preschool Program on Youths Through Age 19.*

ACTIVE LEARNING: MAKING IT WORK

Since children learn from personal interaction with their world, direct experience with real objects, and the application of logical thinking to their experiences, the teacher's role in the High/Scope approach to early childhood education is to provide an environment that promotes active learning and to help children think about their actions. In a sense, children learn by the scientific method of observation and inference, at a level of sophistication corresponding to their development.

To create a setting in which children can become active learners, adults establish and maintain a consistent daily routine that varies only when children have advance notice that things will be different. Field trips, special visits, class-room events, are not surprises. This adherence to routine gives children the control of their time necessary to develop a sense of responsibility and to enjoy the opportunity to be independent.

In the High/Scope Curriculum, the daily routine is a **plan-do-review** sequence that incorporates clean-up and small- and large-group activities. This plan-do-review cycle permits children to make choices about their activities and keeps the teacher intimately involved in the whole process.

Planning time.   Planning time gives children a consistent and structured opportunity to express their ideas to adults and to see themselves as individuals who can make and act on decisions. Children thus experience the power of independence and the joy of working with attentive adults and peers.

In planning time, adults and children assume roles of equal importance. Children discuss their plans with the classroom adults before they carry them out. This helps children form mental images of their ideas, formulate plans of action, and feel confident of success. Adults help children by encouraging and responding to their ideas, suggesting ways to strengthen and extend their plans when appropriate, and understanding and gauging each child's thinking style and level of development. Doing these things during planning time enables adults to know what to look for in the child's activities and to gauge his or her progress. It also helps them anticipate what difficulties children might have and where they might need help.

Work time. The "do" part of the plan-do-review cycle occurs after children have finished planning. It's usually the longest activity period of the day. Since children are responsible for executing their plans, adults do not lead work-time activities. The adult's role during work time is first to observe how children gather information, interact with peers, and solve problems; and second to enter into the children's activities to encourage, extend, and set up problem-solving situations.

Clean-up time. Clean-up time comes after "doing." Children are expected to return materials and equipment to their proper storage places and to put incomplete projects away. Restoring order to the classroom gives children the opportunity to learn and use many basic skills. The classroom must be organized so that children can clean up independently. All classroom materials should be within children's reach on open shelves. Clear labeling, usually a picture, drawing, or outline, enables children to find and return all work materials to their appropriate places.

Recall time. This final phase of the plan-do-review cycle gives children the opportunity to represent their work-time experiences in a variety of developmentally appropriate ways. For example, children may recall the names of the children they involved in their plan, recount the problems they encountered, draw pictures or make models of what they did, review their plan, or verbally describe the activities undertaken. Recall time formally ends the children's planning and work-time activity, although children may go through the cycle more than once if they have time to make another plan.

Small-group time. Small-group time is universally recognized by preschool teachers: the teacher presents an activity in which children participate for a set period of time. Teachers also present structured small-group activities in the High/ Scope Curriculum, but the children contribute their own ideas and solve in their own ways problems presented by the teachers. Small-group activities are drawn from the High/ Scope "key experiences": the children's cultural backgrounds; field trips; seasons of the year; and special age-appropriate projects in cooking, art, science, computers, and so on. Small-group times are geared to the children's needs, abilities, and interests and do not follow a carefully prescribed sequence of lessons. While children are actively involved in exploring and using materials, making choices, and solving problems, the adult extends children's ideas and actions by asking open-ended questions and by setting up additional problem-solving situations.

Large-group circle time. This is the time for all the children to meet together with an adult for ten to fifteen minutes of playing games, singing songs, doing finger plays and basic movement exercises, playing musical instruments, or re-enacting special events. Circle time allows each child to participate in a large group and share the ideas of others.

WHY HIGH/SCOPE'S "KEY EXPERIENCES" ARE SO IMPORTANT

The High/Scope "key experiences" provide a useful framework that guides adults in conducting the classroom program. Key experiences help the teaching staff encourage and extend children's self-chosen activities by providing developmentally appropriate learning experiences. The key experiences free teachers from dependence on standard lesson sequences or activity charts.

Very simple and pragmatic, the key experiences are important to the development of rational thought in children the world over. We have organized them in eight categories:

active learning, using language, representing experiences and ideas, classification, seriation, number concepts, spatial relations, time. Each category is further divided. For example, active learning is subdivided into the following categories: exploring actively with all the senses; discovering relations through direct experience; manipulating, transforming, and combining materials; choosing materials, activities, purposes; acquiring skills with tools and equipment; using the large muscles; taking care of one's own needs.

The key-experience approach structures the High/Scope Curriculum, but is not limiting. This approach allows us to add new experiences as we see fit. For example, we are developing key experiences for music/movement—an area of particular interest to us at this time.

The key experiences also help teachers assess children's developmental progress. By periodically filling out the High/Scope Child Observation Record, which breaks down each of the key experience categories into developmental steps, the teacher can keep track of each child's progress.

WHAT WE WANT FOR PRESCHOOLERS

Perhaps the most difficult lesson any parent or teacher must learn is this: to allow children to live comfortably in their youthful world and to encourage them to discover and follow their self-chosen paths to knowledge and maturity. Our role is to accompany children on their journey, clearing the path of obstacles and offering encouragement and guidance, not surging to the forefront to lead the way.

I've chosen to end this article with a list of High/Scope's basic goals for preschoolers.

1. Develop each child's ability to make choices and decisions about what to do and how to do it, using his or her own time and energy effectively.
2. Develop each child's self-discipline and ability to identify, pursue, and complete self-chosen goals and tasks with originality and responsibility.

3. Develop each child's ability to work with other children and adults in group planning, cooperative efforts, and with shared leadership.

4. Develop each child's knowledge of objects, skill in the arts, and comfort with physical movement.

5. Develop each child's ability to express thoughts, ideas, and feelings; to speak about, dramatize, and graphically represent experiences in order to communicate them to others.

6. Develop each child's ability to comprehend others' spoken, written, dramatic, and graphic representations.

7. Develop each child's ability to apply his or her reasoning abilities to a wide range of situations, using a variety of materials.

8. Develop each child's creativity, initiative, spirit of inquiry, and openness to knowledge and other people's viewpoints.

CHAPTER SEVEN

PARENTS AS FIRST TEACHERS

by Mildred M. Winter

It was Plato who said, "The beginning is half of the whole."
A father of a two-year-old in rural Missouri puts it more
plainly: "A lot of parents just more or less take care of their
kids until they go to school. They expect the teachers to teach
them. But while our children are at home, we are their
teachers at a time when they are learning the most the
fastest."

Few would argue the fact that all the formal education is
influenced by the learning experiences of the first years of life.
Although most parents want the best for their children, few
are adequately prepared for their roles as their child's first
teachers. "You get more information with your new car than
you do with your new baby," says Burton White, an authority
on early childhood development.

As a consequence, too many parents learn the art of child-
rearing and educating the hard way—through trial and error.
As every parent knows, those trials can be trying and those
errors can lead to underachievement and classroom failure.
According to White, relatively few of our children receive as
much education during the first years of life as they might. We

---

*Nearly everyone agrees that parents should be given a larger role in
the education of their preschooler. The Parents as First Teachers
program in Missouri, based on Burton White's work at Harvard, has
developed many strategies to ensure that parents take part successfully. Mildred M. Winter is state program director of the Parents as First
Teacher's project. This article appeared in the May 1985 issue of
Principal magazine.*

need to train parents as teachers, he says, and give them the tools to do the job.

What makes these early years, when the home is the child's school, so critical? Studies in the 1950s and early 1960s by developmental psychologists, as well as by specialists in education and medicine, generally agree on the importance of the first years of life in terms of the development of language, intelligence, and emotional well-being. Studies of early education programs initiated in the 1960s showed that working with the family, rather than bypassing the parents, is the most effective way of helping children get off to the best possible start in life.

Research on the development of children has increased dramatically since 1965, and we now have a much clearer picture of how a child grows and learns in the beginning years, and how the home environment influences that development. The thirteen-year study of early development (1965-78) by the Harvard University Preschool Project contributed significantly to this body of research evidence. The goal of the project, directed by Burton White, was to determine how experiences during the early years influence the development of all major abilities. The extensive observations of children and parent-child interactions in homes representing a variety of educational and economic backgrounds make this study of particular value.

The Harvard study provided fresh insights into the four areas that are the foundations of educational capacity—language, curiosity, social skills, and cognitive intelligence. According to the study, the degree of a child's competence in these four areas at age six can be predicted at age three, with few exceptions. Our education system, however, essentially ignores the formative years, despite the fact that it is very difficult to compensate for a poor beginning with any means we now have available.

To provide a good beginning for their children, the father from rural Missouri and some 300 other families in four of the state's public school districts are now engaged in a unique educational project. The Parents as First Teachers project was implemented in 1981 to provide educational guidance and support for parents during a child's critical years from birth to age three.

The model program is a cooperative effort of the Missouri Department of Elementary and Secondary Education and four school districts—Farmington, Ferguson-Florissant, Francis Howell, and Independence. Departmental grants of $30,000 per site per year have been augmented by in-kind contributions and some local funds. The Danforth Foundation of St. Louis contributed funds for the consultative services of Burton White, who is now director of the Center for Parent Education in Newton, Massachusetts.

The goal of the Parents as First Teachers program is not to create superbabies. Its intent is to demonstrate that education can get children off to the best possible start in school—and life—through a partnership with the home that begins at the onset of learning.

The model program is restricted to first-time parents for two reasons. First, the Harvard Preschool Project found that first-time parents are far more eager for this type of educational support. Second, the effects of the program can be more clearly assessed with new parents and their first-born children than with parents who had previous child-rearing experience and with children who had older siblings.

Each of the four participating school districts was required to recruit a minimum of sixty prospective parents who were expecting their first child between December 1981 and September 1983. The parents were to be broadly representative of new families in each community. It was hoped that at least fifty families per site would remain in the program for the three-year duration of the project. All the districts recruited more than their quotas, with one district enrolling 102.

The recruits represented a broad range of socioeconomic and educational levels from rural, suburban, and urban communities. They included single-parent and two-parent families, families in which both parents worked, and families with either a mother or father at home. The ages of the mothers at the time of birth ranged from sixteen to forty-plus years.

In each school district there was an extensive effort to seek out eligible families in order to avoid a self-selected sample.

Community advisory groups assisted with referrals and recruitment, but personal communication between staff members and prospective parents was an important factor in the final selections.

Parents as First Teachers offers the following services from the third trimester of pregnancy until the child reaches the age of three:

—Information and guidance before the baby is born, to help first-time parents prepare themselves psychologically.

—Information about things to look for and expect in a growing child, and guidance in fostering language, cognitive, social, and motor skill development.

—Periodic checkups of the child's educational and sensory (hearing and vision) development to detect possible problems or handicaps. If serious problems are discovered, help is sought from other agencies or professionals.

—A parent resource center, located in a school building, which provides a meeting place for parents and staff, and facilities for child care during parent meetings.

—Monthly hour-long private visits in the home or at the center to individualize the education program for each family.

—Monthly group meetings with other new parents to share experiences and discuss topics of interest.

Personnel at each district site include a district administrator who provides overall program supervision in addition to other duties, a teacher-director, a parent educator, and a part-time clerk-typist. The teacher-director, who is also a parent, is responsible for program planning and materials development, and shares responsibility for home visits and group meetings with the parent educator. Both are trained in child development and early childhood education, and are skilled in working with adults.

Each of the sites also includes an advisory committee made up of health-care and social-service professionals, as well as representatives of religious and civic organizations. These committees have helped to build a broad base of community awareness, involvement, and support. A state supervisory committee provides guidance to the program.

Parents as First Teachers seems to be working. Parent responses to questionnaires and telephone interviews by an independent evaluation team indicate that families highly value the services they are receiving and are proud of their children's accomplishments. The best evidence of parent enthusiasm for the program may well be the low attrition rate.

Families openly credit the project with reducing the stress and increasing the pleasure of child-rearing. Although not designed as a child abuse prevention program, the project addresses some of the root causes of abuse—unrealistic expectations, inability to cope, low self-esteem, and social isolation. Teenage parents living in multi-generational homes are often provided biweekly home visits to help them through difficult times.

Comprehensive testing of project children is done as close as possible to the children's third birthdays, even though each child's progress has been monitored by parent and educator since birth. Any minor or major problems receive prompt attention, and the project has been particularly watchful for any indications of hearing loss that could impede the progress of language development.

The participating school districts stand to benefit from this investment in several ways. They expect the program to have a carry-over effect on the project children's self-esteem and positive attitudes toward learning when they enter school. They also anticipate improved academic achievement and a reduced need for remedial education. The development of trust and good will between parents and professional educators, based on mutual concern for the young child, bodes well for a continuing positive home-school relationship during the school years.

Programs patterned after Parents as First Teachers are now being implemented in other school districts through use of local school budgets or federal funds. Parents as First Teachers will become the model for parent education in school districts across Missouri under the Early Childhood Development Act passed in 1984. Parent education for all parents of children under the age of three who wish to participate is authorized for state funding by this bill. When he was governor, Christopher Bond, who became a father for the first time at age forty, was instrumental in getting this legislation passed.

Early childhood education programs such as this, which affect the total well-being of the child, have benefited from resources outside of education that are concerned about family life. In Missouri, Commissioner of Education Arthur Mallory appointed prominent Missourians to a Committee on Parents as Teachers. Responding to the challenge to promote parent involvement in their children's education, this group has successfully raised money from foundations and the corporate sector to fund training of parent educators.

The state's leading marketing service company, which is represented on the committee, has developed and made available to school districts a Parents as First Teachers Marketing Plan. The plan tailors messages and steps for program implementation for the different groups within a community that stand to benefit in some way from the program. This same company also produced and donated multiple copies of an audiovisual presentation for dissemination to a broad range of audiences in the state.

Even without a state initiative, some form of Missouri's Parents as First Teachers program could be implemented in most school districts throughout the country. A congratulatory message from a school on the birth of a child would be a modest beginning and a pleasant surprise for most families. A visit by an administrator, teacher, or trained volunteer to deliver information on child development and early learning would be an effective follow-up. An invitation might be extended to participate in get-togethers with other new parents involving topics of mutual interest. There are people in every school and community who have valuable information to share with parents of young children, and who can listen and respond to their concerns.

A corner of the school library might be allocated to parents for articles and books on parenting and recommended books for reading aloud to children. A display or lending library of commercial and homemade toys that have child appeal and also foster learning at different ages would be of interest. "Make-it-and-take-it" toy workshops are always popular.

Many of the current efforts toward educational reform appear to be targeted to the wrong end of the continuum. The present practice of spending increasingly larger amounts of money on children's programs through twelve years of school, beginning at age six, is inconsistent with what we know about human development. Missouri, in conducting what one major newspaper calls "A quiet revolution in education," has taken a significant step in the other direction. Providing families with timely, practical information they can use in teaching their young children and fostering optimal development may be the wisest and least expensive investment that can be made to improve our schools.

CHAPTER EIGHT

HOW TO FIND A GOOD DAY-CARE PROGRAM

by Richard C. Endsley and Marilyn R. Bradbard

Perhaps each reader of this article accepts the view that parents can and should contribute to the enhancement of the quality of day care. Yet, unfortunately, the fight for better day care in this country has centered on elements in the day-care system other than parent involvement (e.g., staff training, licensing). Even the subject of parent involvement *after* a child has entered a day-care program, which has a secure base of support, remains largely unexploited by researchers, program developers, and practitioners.

But what about parent involvement before choosing a day-care program? After all, a child does not enroll in a particular high-quality day-care program unless his or her parents choose it. In most instances and for most families, there are options from among equally affordable and accessible programs that do (and probably always will) vary in quality. Therefore we believe that one of the prime, yet overlooked, tasks for family and day-care professionals is to reach parents

How should parents choose the right day-care and pre-school settings for their children? In this chapter, the results of an experiment designed to prepare parents to make good choices are reviewed. This report was originally published as part of the High/Scope Early Childhood Papers, *No. 3, by the High/Scope Educational Research Foundation.*

with information and tools for selecting day care. This effort should bring the pressures of informed choice into the day-care marketplace as well as into the sociopolitical debates about meeting parents' child care needs.

In the interest of pursuing the role of parents as day-care consumers, we have embarked on a study of the processes that parents go through as they choose day care, the criteria they use, and the characteristics of those parents who are apparently more successful than others in finding good programs. We also have attempted to establish that parents can become more effective and discriminating day-care consumers by having information available that will improve their day-care selection. Our results are limited to the kinds of families (mostly middle class) and kind of day care (proprietary) to which we have had access.

HOW DO PARENTS CHOOSE DAY CARE?

Our research grew from our alarm over the rather casual comments of the first few parents we interviewed. We recall the wife of a military officer who said she simply chose a center by opening the Yellow Pages, closing her eyes, and "letting her fingers do the walking." Where her fingers stopped was where she called and subsequently enrolled her child. Similarly, we recall the college professor who stated that his choice was based on his eyes being open at the right time—that is, he saw the center as he passed it every day on his way to work. His choice apparently gave no consideration to the fact that four or five other centers were within five minutes driving time. Perhaps more important, one of these centers may have been superior to, and less costly than, the one he chose.

Our early alarm gave way to a more balanced view. In phone interviews with eighty-six parents, we found only one who used the Yellow Pages "roulette approach" to selecting day care. Still, the evidence indicated that few parents were well-informed or very systematic in their search. For example, nearly 10 percent said they had made their choice without first visiting the centers in which they ultimately enrolled their children. Of the remainder, who did visit the centers first, only one third also had visited other programs to "comparison-shop." Further, while from the total group of parents we generated a long list of appropriate things they claimed to have done on their visits to centers (e.g., observing children, caregivers, toys; asking questions about meals, discipline), only two of these were listed, on average, per parent. As a result, important considerations and procedures were overlooked by many parents. For example, only about two-thirds of the parents stated that they talked to the directors, and only about one-third said they observed the children.

We had deliberately selected a group of well-educated parents (mostly college graduates) whose children were attending programs judged by local experts to be at least average or above in quality. We assumed that our results would therefore provide a conservative estimate of parents' superficiality, randomness, and lack of concern with the day-care selection process. But these parents were clearly concerned about quality, even if they were not sure about how to evaluate it. For instance, most of them said they would have greatly appreciated having more information and listed as most important the program's educational benefits and the competencies of the staff. These parents were at least concerned about, and aware of, the importance of a good program; what they lacked was information on how to distinguish good programs from others.

WHICH PARENTS ARE SUCCESSFUL IN SELECTING HIGH-QUALITY DAY CARE?

While it became clear to us that parents need more information, we were also interested in the state of affairs of the more typical parent. What is it about these parents that leads some of them to choose a higher-quality program than others? We obtained both demographic information and information on the day-care selection process from a set of 257 parents whose children attended any one of eighteen proprietary day-care centers located in four Southeastern communities (three small college towns and one small mill town). The parents generally had a high school education, and their average educational attainment was two years beyond high school. As before, the quality of the centers had been independently assessed by local day-care experts—day-care professionals who were very familiar with the programs but were not aware of the purpose of our study. Using a 9-point rating scale supplemented by an observation guide, the experts rate the programs as ranging from 2.5 points (e.g., licensed but providing minimal custodial care) to 7.5 points (e.g., developmentally based program lacking only comprehensive services and ideal child-caregiver ratio), with most judged to fall between 4 and 6 points (slightly below to slightly above average).

In general, the results supported the role and value of parents having information and exhibiting care in deliberating over this information. For example, those who chose higher quality programs had read more about day care and had been more likely to talk to professionals and get their advice (although few were able to do this). Even though the well-educated parents in the preceding study did not appear very systematic, it was noteworthy that in this second study, the best single predictor of choosing quality in day care was the parents' educational level, particularly the educational level of the husband. Job status, which along with education forms the other half of the conventional index of socioeconomic status (SES), was much less predictive than education. Further, education and job status combined were a less reliable predictor of choosing quality in day care.

Educational level reflected the parents' thoughtfulness and skills for getting access to information (i.e., reading about day care or contacting professionals). Even more likely, it was a reflection of the parents' value systems—that is, whether they valued education. Parents with a high level of education generally value education and consequently could be interested in one of the main components defining high-quality day care—the educational component. This could lead to their more consistent selection of quality in programs.

We should be clear that the link between good day-care choices and parents' educational level was not a social status phenomenon. That is, parents who were better educated did not live on the "right side of town" and consequently enroll their children in a better center near their homes; nor did parents who were less educated live on the "wrong side of town" and enroll their children in poorer centers in their part of town. Education was not an index of family income that led more educated parents (and parents who earn more money) to the programs that also cost more. In our sample there was no correlation between day-care center quality and location or cost. In fact, there was little variation in cost in our sample ($27-34 per week per child in 1980 dollars).

After the appropriate statistical adjustments were made, there were four other factors in addition to parents' education that emerged as independent and significant predictors of parents' selecting quality day care. These were (a) dissatisfaction with previous child-care arrangements; (b) wives and husbands discussing the day-care decision together; (c) choosing centers based on their location (a negative predictor); and (d) size of family (also a negative predictor). Briefly, if parents had previous experiences of dissatisfaction with child care, they were more likely to choose a higher quality center. Apparently, just having a previous child-care arrangement wasn't enough—it had to be one in which the parents had some problems and dissatisfaction, resulting in a more careful search by them the next time.

Also, when husbands and wives discussed the day-care decision together (85 percent were currently married), better choices of a center (i.e., the center was rated better by experts) seemed to be forthcoming. As might be expected, many mothers are given the whole responsibility of the day-care decision. About six of the ten mothers in our sample had discussed the issue with their spouses; the other four had not. We did not have the impression that the fathers who were involved in the decision had been active in seeking out information about local centers. Rather, we suspect that the importance of their consultation with their wives was in providing them with psychological support and in sharing commitment to the family decision that the wife would find quality day care.

Of the two negative predictors, one was expected and one

was not. We expected to find that parents who used the location of the center as a criterion in choosing day care (recall our college professor) would tend to make a poorer choice, and they did. It should be pointed out that in the communities we studied, no parent was more than twenty minutes (and most were not more than ten minutes) from any day-care center. Thus location should not have been an important criterion for these parents.

The unexpected finding was that the greater the number of children in a family, the less likely were the parents to choose a high-quality program. This surprised us, since we assumed the more children, the more experience and expertise the parents might have had in choosing quality in child-care arrangements. Two factors about this finding make it of more than passing interest: First, the parents in this study generally had small families (mean of 1.6 children). In fact, less than 10 percent had more than two children, and the five largest families had only four children. Yet, the effect was clearly significant and was due largely to the poorer choices made by parents with three or four children.

HELPING PARENTS CHOOSE HIGH QUALITY DAY CARE

While parents often may be motivated to find the highest-quality day-care arrangements, they are often severely limited by a lack of knowledge and information to help them make the best decisions. In an effort to provide them with one source of information, we developed and field-tested the Parent Guide to Quality Day-Care Centers—a list of items that parents observe in a short twenty- to thirty-minute visit to a day-care center. Briefly we went through three major steps in developing the Guide:

Step 1. Based on our review of the child development/day-care literature, we generated a set of items consisting of characteristics parents should and could see when visiting a high-quality day-care center. These items included (a) *health and safety features* (e.g., electrical outlets are covered with safety caps); (b) *adult-child and* *child-child interactions* (e.g., adults are observed praising children, saying such things as "you did a good job putting away the toys"); (c) *program activities* (e.g, attractive and well-written story and picture books are available to the children); (d) *home-center coordination* (e.g., the center posts a sign encouraging parents or those involved in child care at home to visit the center at any time during the day); and (e) *physical space* (e.g., the center has an individual space, such as locker, drawer, cubbie, box, or coat hook, for each child to store belongings).

Eighteen day-care/child-development professionals, many with national reputations, examined our list of items, to determine whether they were clearly worded, reflected high quality, and could be observed in a center during a single twenty- to thirty-minute visit. Finally, a group of mothers examined the items for their clarity and potential for being observed in a short twenty- to thirty-minute visit to a center. This process resulted in a sixty-five–item checklist.

Step 2.   The second step involved field testing the Guide. Initially, a group of five local day-care experts independently rated twelve licensed proprietary day-care centers on a 9-point quality scale, where 1 point represented a "deplorable" program that should not be licensed; 5 points, an "average" program; and 9 points, a "superior" program with comprehensive services.[1] Reassuringly, the experts were in high agreement (mean correlation among the experts was .82) about the quality of each program; most programs were judged to be a point above or a point below the average score of 5.

Then twenty-six working and/or student women (white, with three years of college) were asked to visit four of the twelve centers: two centers somewhat below average and two centers somewhat above average (as judged by the local experts). Using the Guide, the women made some visits in pairs and returned to some centers a week later, thereby providing us with information on how consistent (reliable) the women would be with themselves and each other in what they saw in each center. The reliability of the instrument

[1]It was illuminating for us to discover in a college community with literally scores of professionals in the fields of child development, early childhood education, and day care, that only five persons could be uncovered who not only had enough training but also had enough first-hand knowledge of the local programs to be able to evaluate them. Thus, we have concluded that truly informed professionals are not likely to be available to most parents in most communities.

proved to be quite satisfactory—that is, all observer agreements exceeded 75 percent. But most important, their observations indicated that they saw substantially more positive Guide items in higher quality centers than in poorer quality centers.

Step 3. The final phase of Guide development and testing involved asking twenty-eight working women (white, with three years of college) to visit the same centers. It should be pointed out that all these women were potential day-care "consumers" (twenty-two were already mothers). That is, they were actively seeking day care or said that they would be seeking day care in the future. Each woman rated the centers on the 9-point quality scale used by the local experts. However, only half of the women visited the centers with the Guide, while the other half went without the Guide. As expected, the results revealed that those women who had the Guide in hand when they visited the centers made judgments of quality that were very close to those of the experts. More important, they significantly differentiated the higher and lower quality groups of centers, while those who made judgments without the Guide did not, generally rating them all as average.

In sum, we were pleased to find that our sample of interested, reasonably well-educated mothers were able to distinguish between somewhat below-average and somewhat above-average proprietary day-care centers simply by having available an easy-to-use list of items that professionals and other mothers judged to be characteristic of high-quality day care. Since our initial field testing of the Guide, we have again tested it in another community, with very similar results (see Bradbard & Endsley, 1982). Further, the Guide (in somewhat revised form), the rationale for the items that form the Guide, and information on how parents can be involved in their children's day-care program after the children are enrolled, were the basis for our book, *Quality Day Care: A Handbook of Choices for Parents and Caregivers*, published by Prentice-Hall (Spectrum) in 1981.

HELPING PARENTS HELP THEMSELVES: OTHER WAYS

We would like to close this paper with some suggestions for professionals in the day-care field, suggestions that are straightforward implications of the results of our research:

Provide parents with do-it-yourself guides and reading. Our
Guide is one of several available to parents today. One of the
best can be obtained from the U.S. Department of Health and
Human Services (1980). (See Appendix.) This guide, which is
very similar to our own, seems to be a potentially valuable
resource for parents.

In any case, our research on the day-care selection process
has led us to believe that parents who simply read about day
care select better quality programs. Thus, perhaps having any
kind of day-care guide or reading material in hand, as compared to having no resource material at all, may make parents
sensitive to the myriad things to consider in selecting a
program. Yet, we wonder how many professionals suggest
guides, checklists, or reading materials to parents who ask for
help in selecting day care.

In 1979 we surveyed state day-care licensers about the
kinds of information they provided parents who called asking
for help with day-care selection. Twenty-five percent of the
licensers representing the fifty states and the District of
Columbia said they either could not or did not suggest reading
material to parents to help them make more informed day-
care decisions. We think that day-care professionals could
offer a very valuable service to parents by having day-care
guides and reading materials available or suggesting specific
sources where these materials could be obtained.

Build parents' knowledge and confidence. This brings us to
another interesting point. Traditionally, licensers have viewed
their role as maintaining a minimum standard of quality below
which centers are not allowed to operate. Licensers in several
states have challenged this viewpoint and have tried to develop standards that exceed the minimum and provide more
help to parents who need information on how to select day
care. Yet the more normal state of affairs is that most licensers (not to mention other professionals) still give parents who
request information little more than a list of licensed centers
in their locale. Occasionally, they may also provide a copy of
the licensing standards, but these documents are often legalis-
tic and difficult for the average parent to interpret; they

typically concentrate on many health and safety details that extend beyond the interests of most parents. Consequently, many parents to whom we have spoken have been very frustrated by the "I can't tell you anything more" attitude of licensers.

We are not suggesting that licensers and other child-care information and referral specialists tell parents which centers they think are the good ones or the bad ones, though this type of evaluative information is often provided. On the contrary, we feel very strongly that parents should *not* depend heavily on the advice of others; rather, they should visit centers themselves, evaluate and weigh the information they obtain in those centers, and then make their own day-care decision. The problem is that parents often do not have enough information to know that they should not listen solely to other people's second-hand (and often inaccurate) information but that they can (and should) read about day care, go to visit several centers, and comparison-shop with a checklist in hand. Licensers and other professionals need to take the time to explain to parents why they cannot tell them which centers are the best. Then they need to build parents' confidence to make them feel competent enough for a systematic search of the available day care in their community.

Break down the day-care search into smaller components. As professionals, we know that the day-care selection process should involve many components, from the time parents decide to select a center until the time the child is actually enrolled. For example, they must decide whether part-time or full-time care is needed and whether the care is to be provided in a center, by a babysitter, or by a family day-care provider. Further, parents must decide how much they can afford to pay for care, how many centers are located close enough to home to make them likely choices, and whether the quality of care provided in each arrangement is acceptable.

These day-care selection components can all be broken down into smaller components. For example, we know that when parents visit a day-care center, they should talk to the center director and as many caregivers as possible; ask specific questions about policies (e.g., insurance, meals, diaper service, discipline, educational philosophy, hours of operation); observe the general interactions of children and caregivers; observe activities and equipment, both indoors and outdoors; observe how and whether parent involvement takes place; and so on.

In short, day-care selection can look like a very complicated process to a parent unless that parent can be "walked through" the process verbally or with written materials. Since most parents are not aware of the various components that should be included in the day-care selection process, we would like to encourage professionals who have contacts with parents to first ask questions that break down the day-care selection process into smaller, less complicated components (e.g., What are the various types of child care available to you? How many centers are in your locale? How many of these centers offer full-day care?). Then professionals should point out to parents that each component and subcomponent is important (e.g., when you visit centers, be sure to do all of the following: talk to the director, talk to all caregivers who will work with your child, observe child-child interactions, observe caregiver-child interactions, observe activities, etc.).

Make parents aware of variables that are related to choosing quality day care. Based on the findings of our research, we think professionals should explore with parents whether they have used previous child-care arrangements, whether they were satisfied or dissatisfied with them, and the significance of their dissatisfaction as a predictor of selecting quality day care. Similarly, parents could be made aware that discussing the day-care decision with a spouse or perhaps another person in their social network usually results in a better decision.

Next, professionals can warn parents that selecting day care based on location, cost, or other convenience factors may not lead them to select quality day care. Parents should know that within certain locales there may be several centers of similar quality and that the relative quality of these centers cannot always be predicted by their costs. This is particularly true in the case of middle-class parents who are often re-

stricted to proprietary day-care arrangements; these are precisely the programs in which quality levels are the most
difficult to determine because they are often just below or just
above average.

Finally, parents might be interested in knowing about our
finding that those families with one or two children may be
more likely to select better quality day care than families with
three or four children. This finding, and our speculations
about it, could have the effect of sensitizing parents with a
greater number of children to not be too casual about selecting
and managing their children's out-of-home day-care experiences.

In effect, we are suggesting a compatible alternative to the
types of advice that licensers and other information and
referral specialists typically offer parents who are in the
process of selecting child care. It is neither adequate nor
appropriate to simply provide parents with a list of licensed
child-care centers or a copy of licensing standards (as licensers generally do), or to tell parents which specific programs
are good, average, or poor (as information and referral specialists sometimes do). Instead, we propose that professionals
should educate parents about, and more fully involve parents
in, the child-care selection process by (a) providing them with
easy-to-use guides and reading materials, (b) building their
confidence so they feel competent enough to make a systematic search of the available child care, (c) breaking down the
selection process into smaller components and "walking
through" the process with parents either verbally or with
written materials, and (d) making parents aware of the various
factors that may lead some parents to select better quality
care than others.

In short, we believe that child-care professionals should
take a more active part in helping parents to better appreciate
their role as the crucial link between their child's and the
family's needs and the delivery of high-quality child-care
services.

CHAPTER NINE

LEARNING AT HOME

by Donald Graves and Virginia Stuart

Laws mandating school attendance imply that children can learn more in school than they can at home. Most people believe, for example, that teachers are better equipped to teach basic language skills than parents—especially parents in the lower income brackets. Convinced that these parents could not provide what their children needed, the United States Congress established the Head Start program in 1965 to give preschool children oral-language "enrichment." The British, who also equated financial with linguistic disadvantages, instituted a similar program.

British researcher Gordon Wells challenges the assumptions underlying such programs. In an ambitious study of language development, he analyzed 1280 recordings of spontaneous conversation in the homes of 128 British preschoolers from all levels of society. Wells and his research team followed thirty-two of the children into the early grades of elementary school, gathering recordings of their conversations in the classroom. He found that the home, more than the school, gives children opportunities to practice talking and to learn from their conversations with adults. In the homes he

---

This chapter is an exploration of how parents can nurture reading and writing skills in their preschoolers. It suggests that good early education depends largely on a teaching style that includes encouragement and play and avoids pushing and "instruction." This material is from the book Write from the Start: Tapping Your Child's Natural Writing Ability, *published in 1985 by E. P. Dutton. Donald Graves is a professor of education at the University of New Hampshire; Virginia Stuart teaches writing there.*

studied, children spoke more often, started more conversations, drew more responses from adults, asked more questions, and used more complete sentences and complex syntax than they did at school. In an article in *Theory into Practice,* Gordon Wells and Jan Wells conclude that "there were no homes that did not provide richer opportunities than the schools we observed for learning through talk with an adult." And all the children became competent speakers before they reached school age.

Parents seem to have a natural ability to help small children learn how to talk. In fact, when it comes to talking with children, many teachers would do well to take a cue from parents, or even from their own behavior with children at home. In his study, Wells found that differences in parents' conversational styles were highly correlated with the rate of oral-language development in preschool children. He was able to identify the characteristics that mark the kind of interaction that helps children most. Some parents in his study were much more likely than others to pick up on something a child had said and expand on it, affirming the child's meaning and developing it further. But all the parents used this collaborative style more than the teachers he observed. So the difference between home and school is partly a matter of numbers but largely a matter of style.

In his book *Learning through Interaction,* Wells offers a brief conversation between a mother and her two-year-old son Mark as an example of the kind of talk that helps children learn. The child has just drawn his mother's attention to some birds, which he sometimes calls "jubs," outside in the garden.

"Birds, Mummy," he says.

His mother responds with "Mm."

"Jubs," says Mark.

"What are they doing?" his mother asks.

"Jubs bread."

"Oh, look, they're eating the berries, aren't they?"

"Yeah."

"That's their food," the mother adds. "They have berries for dinner."

"Oh."

Wells's example is rudimentary because the child is so young; yet it includes the kernel of a whole attitude toward children and learning. In short, it represents a mother's belief that her child wants to learn. To help him do that, she draws out what he already knows and helps him add to that knowledge.

For better or worse, parents are still the most influential teachers their children will ever have. Too often parents think they must mimic teachers, who work with twenty-six children. Even teachers don't teach with one child as they do with an entire class. But the teaching role at home is different. Parents teach by listening to their children and helping them gain control over what they already know. Parents teach by reading and writing to their children. Children also learn by watching their parents solving problems, writing, and reading.*

Children's ability to talk, listen, read, and write will have a lifelong effect on their ability to learn. In turn, parents have a profound influence on the development of those skills during the preschool years and beyond. Parents can develop children's love for reading and writing in concert with, or in spite of, schooling. Expanding on their own natural strength, a knack for conversing with children, parents can help children to use their own knowledge and add to it through reading and writing. And if they don't try to be imitation teachers, parents can have a lot of fun in the process.

Laying the Groundwork

One day my daughter Laura was teaching her three-year-old niece Margaret how to set the table. First, Laura put the spoon and knife on the right side and the fork on the left side of the plate. Then she said to Margaret, "Now, you do the next one." So Margaret put the fork and the spoon on the right side with the knife on the left side of the plate. Laura then said, "Oh, Marga-

---

*Donald Graves's comments are in italics.

ret, I forgot to tell you that the spoon and the knife are friends. The fork already knows them, but they're not really very good friends. So the fork stays over here, but the spoon and knife just love to talk." That was the end of that episode.

The next morning, Margaret set the table again. This time she put the fork on the left side and the knife and the spoon on the right, but the handle of the spoon was facing up toward the blade of the knife. Then Laura said, "You've got it just right. But they can't talk even though they're right next to each other. Now, if you turn the spoon around so that his head is up instead of down by the knife's feet, then they can talk."

Without realizing it, Laura had used a technique psychologist Jerome Bruner calls "scaffolding." The temporary structures parents use to help a child learn resemble the scaffolding contractors erect around a building as they follow its growth upward. But often the scaffold has to keep changing as it adapts to the actual structure that it surrounds. In short, the scaffold exists for the building, not the building for the scaffold. The child doesn't exist for the parent so the parent can be a teacher. The parent exists for the child that the child may learn, and if the child learns, then the parent will.

In her lesson on table setting, Laura followed Margaret. Laura introduced the information, and then when the child went another way, Laura transformed her language to fit Margaret's own understanding. She had to adjust twice so that Margaret, in turn, could come up with her own version, using the language given to her.

The two episodes contained most of the elements of good teaching. Laura gave a demonstration. She used language that tied her lesson to information the child already had and simplified her presentation so Margaret could focus on just the information she needed. Laura also gave Margaret a chance to practice and corrected her without making her feel bad. Most important, it was all done in the spirit of play. The one missing element was role reversal, in which Margaret demonstrates something for Laura. But that's more advanced.

The same principles underlying Laura's lesson and Mark's conversation with his mother can be applied to conversations with children of all ages. With older children, parents can ask more questions and encourage more role reversals. Like teachers, parents can help children become more conscious of the things they do know and of the ways in which they learn. Thus children become independent—eager and able to learn more on their own.

Parents help children learn by showing them how to do things. When a child does something successfully, the parent confirms what the child has done. "Oh, I didn't know that you knew how to take a chain off the bicycle, get it in the right gear, and then put it back on," a father might say to his daughter. "How did you learn to do that?" Thus, he has made it possible for the child to explain how she knows what she knows. But he is also showing that people can ask other people how they know how to do things. Before long, the child reverses the role and asks the father how he has just managed to do something.

Parents also help a child learn through the language they use. When a mother shows her son how to build a fire in the woodstove, she uses the appropriate vocabulary: "air space," "draft," "vent," and "buffle." Thus she has given the boy the language he needs to talk about stoves and to get more information about them when she isn't there.

When people perceive themselves as knowledgeable, they want to learn more. People who think they know nothing often work hard to impress others with their knowledge, as opposed to listening to what others might have to teach them. People who are secure in what they know see no need to compete. They can just plain enjoy learning from other people.

It is the parent's role to help children to know what they know, to help them establish their own territory. Someone's territory is the area of knowledge or expertise for which that person becomes known. My own son, Bill, for example, has had a love affair with the Civil

War. He became interested in it when he was in first grade and was still pursuing it when he graduated from high school. But he put his own twist on it by becoming a rabid rebel, a disciple of the Southern cause, even though we lived in the North. That established the uniqueness of his territory still more. Not that he was in favor of slavery, but he did admire military prowess.

He studied the battles, knew all of the generals on both sides, and could show the stupidity of politically appointed Northern generals. For him, the Southern cause was ground he knew he could easily defend and win. A child who establishes an area of knowledge like that will continue to read about it, write about it, and teach other people about it.

Some parents help a child establish territory, but for all the wrong reasons. A father may develop his son's interest in fishing in order to create a fishing companion. That's all right as long as the father seeks to bring out what's unique in the boy's fishing knowledge and experience. But parents sometimes give children knowledge in order to use it against them, by implying that "everything you ever learned came from me and always will." The territory, in that case, has the parents' fingerprints all over it.

At home or in the classroom, I want children to have outright title to the territories that interest them. That's a little hard at first, because buyers never own the land or house right away. The bank does. But over time, through experience and the help of others, people gradually learn what it is to be an owner and, finally, a responsible one.

THE PARENTAL MODEL

At the end of his ten-year study of language development in Briston, England, Gordon Wells examined the link between preschool experiences and abilities, and later success in primary school. Although oral-language skill proved to be highly correlated with school attainment, he identified an even stronger predictor of success: "knowledge of literacy." (So few of the preschoolers he studied did any writing at home that Wells was unable to draw any correlation there at all.)

In other words, the preschoolers who are most likely to succeed are those who come to first grade equipped with a familiarity with the written word. They know which way to hold a book, for example, and where to find the words. But that's not all they know. It is likely that this acquaintance with the superficial features of the act of reading signifies a much deeper understanding of the purpose of reading. Children who have been read to know that words carry meaning. Children who have not been read to may not be aware that written words are meaningful. And the endless exercises that fill workbooks may reinforce their misunderstanding.

Wells believes that storybooks help preschool children in an even broader way by introducing them to imaginary worlds they wouldn't otherwise encounter. As he puts it, they develop the ability to "disembed" themselves from the specific world of the here and now. That ability, he believes, forms a bridge to the other imaginary or abstract realms found in academic disciplines such as history, science, mathematics, or literature.

Thus, as many parents realize, reading aloud to children can make strong contributions to their future success as students. Reading aloud also makes children want to hear more and, eventually, read more by themselves. Parents may have better luck with motivating young readers than teachers do, simply because bookstores, libraries, and many homes are filled with good children's books that are well-written and enjoyable to read. Schools, on the other hand, often limit children to insipid basal readers.

Many parents, nevertheless, fail to instill a love of reading in their children. Despite frequent reading-aloud sessions during their early years, these children often lose interest in books during the middle grades. Given the quality of the reading materials and instruction in many classrooms, this loss of interest should come as no surprise. But most parents make no effort to reverse the process. They stop reading aloud, even though children of all ages, as well as adults, can take pleasure in listening. Parents may also be unaware of the effect their own reading habits have on older children.

Nathan, the son of a farmer, and Sarah, the daughter of a doctor, were fifth-grade classmates. One day, Sarah came home and told her mother, "I can see why Nathan is so smart; because he reads all the time at school. Every spare minute he has, he reads." The next time the two mothers met, Sarah's mother commented on Nathan's interest in reading and added, "I don't understand why our children don't read more. We read quite a lot, and we're interested in books and literature. We have a lot of books around the house.

"Do the children ever see you reading?" Nathan's mother asked.

As she thought about it, Sarah's mother realized that she and her husband did practically all of their reading when the children were out of the house or in bed. In Nathan's family, on the other hand, both parents read off and on throughout the day. Nathan's father came home in midmorning for his second breakfast and at noontime for dinner, and he always had a fat book on the table next to his easy chair. Nathan's parents often discussed things they had read in front of the children. In short, both parents read voraciously, and both children read voraciously.

When it comes to reading, first-grader Kasey McGarrigle has acquired not only her father's appetite but also his tastes. Ed McGarrigle loves fantasy and science fiction. Kasey has often seen both her parents reading. "When she sees that," her father says, "she trusts that we wouldn't be doing it just to waste our time. She realizes there's probably something in there that's treasurelike, whether it's a fantasy or another world or a character she can relate to. She's looking for things in books. And it's funny—I know she's a page-counter like me. She really likes the satisfaction of having read. 'I read twenty pages,' she'll say." When the little girl visits a friend or goes on any overnight trip, she carries her current book in her suitcase.

Parents who want their children to read and write must read and write themselves—and talk about the experience. The principle is so simple that even a six-year-old could understand it. One six-year-old who did was the little boy named Nathaniel, author of "Why Children Like Their Mom Better Than Their Dad." In a piece called "Kids Thd Whit" (Kids Should Write), he speculated on the reason why they don't: "Thy Doont Whit be Cus Thy wont to be liuk Thr MOM and Thr Muthur's Doont Whit." (They don't write because they want to be like their mom and their mothers don't write.) Nathaniel himself doesn't get to write much at school. He does have the occasional assignment, such as "write about your pet" (a difficult one for children who, like Nathaniel, have no pets). But he does most of his writing at home, whenever he feels like it. He often feels like it after his mother or his older sister Meg has written something. He wrote "Kids Thd Whit" shortly after his mother wrote an article. He wanted to write an article, too. Not long after the children's grandfather wrote a letter to the editor of a newspaper, fourth-grader Meg wrote a letter to the state governor, recommending the installation of seat belts in school buses. She also sent copies of the letter to two local newspapers.

Sometimes children inspire their parents to write. In one family, both parents began keeping journals after their son started writing in school. That child was lucky—his experiences at home and school were mutually reinforcing. Other parents often become inspired to write for, or to, their children. A surprise note in the lunchbox is nearly always well-received and usually answered. Parents with a stronger interest in writing may enjoy composing their own children's stories or making a gift of a piece of writing.

About ten years ago, I wrote a piece for each of my children—as well as for my mother, father, and wife—on their birthdays. I just sat and wrote several pages of vignettes of very special moments between us. I didn't realize it at the time, but I was trying to give them a mirror image of how special they were to me and to the family. Last Christmas, I tried to put together everything I could remember about all the Christmases we had had together from the time when I was first engaged to Betty. Then I wrote a Christmas book full of all those memories.

Parents who read and write not only demonstrate that those activities are an enjoyable part of life, they also demonstrate the process that they go through when they read and write. Children who hear their parents reading aloud to one another or arguing about the interpretation of a letter from the government see that reading is something to share, interpret, and discuss. A child who sees a parent crossing out lines and crumpling up paper understands that writing is a process that may go through several stages before completion. When Susan Stires took a trip to Indiana, she received a letter from her younger daughter, who had just finished first grade. "She not only sent me the final copy, which was written in Magic Marker and highly decorated on a paper towel in perfect printing," Stires recalls, "but she also sent me her draft—she knows that I'm as interested in her draft as I am in her final copy."

Most parents enjoy work or a hobby that requires a creative approach, whether painting, repairing cars, writing computer programs, playing the guitar, training horses, cooking from scratch, or even shopping for clothes to name just a few examples. These parents can help their children see the similarities between such activities and the process of writing, the need for cultivating unexpected ideas, entertaining alternatives, accepting failure, and being persistent. Unless parents draw attention to these parallels, however, children may miss them, especially if schooling instills a get-it-right-the-first-time mentality. Joan Tornow, for instance, grew up in a home where she was constantly exposed to the creative process on a high level. Her father, Leland C. Clark, Jr., invented the artificial heart-lung machine and artificial blood among other things. Tornow remembers seeing him rush into the kitchen with ten pounds of fresh spinach one day. He chopped it up, boiled it, and then dried it in front of a fan, all in search of an enzyme that would help measure lactic acid in the blood. The enzyme he extracted from the spinach worked, but not well enough. Four years later, he found the enzyme he needed.

The spinach incident was just one of many. Yet despite her father's repeated and graphic demonstrations of the creative process of working by trial and error, Tornow held herself to a different set of standards when she wrote. "I used to think that all my scribbled drafts were something to be ashamed of," she says. "They were like your slip showing. It seemed that you should have gotten it right the first time, and I always thought of that as an indication of inferiority." When she took a class on teaching writing, she began to see the connection between her father's process of discovery in medicine and the process of discovery in writing.

As important as the example parents set through their activities is their attitude toward those activities and toward members of the family. Although it is good to read to children, listen to children, and write to children, the energy for doing those things comes from my own view of their importance. I stress importance because there are countless examples of illiterate people who valued literacy, rejoiced in their children and in each other and, in fact, raised children who grew up to be highly literate. On the other hand, I've seen people who religiously read to their children and raised them with a book in hand but failed to laugh and enjoy them.

The important thing is to enjoy your children and, above all, to find things you and your spouse enjoy doing and learning. Parents need to help themselves and each other as much as they help their children. Husbands and wives need to develop their own territories and interests. They must share their own knowledge and experiences with each other because children will be observing that model for a long time. That's the only one they'll have. If between husband and wife, one works hard to show how dumb the other one is, that model also can be infectious to the children. So, any consideration of literacy within the family falls on the backdrop of the enjoyment of people and learning and oneself.

THE OPPORTUNITY TAKEN

When Adi Rule was three, her favorite book was *Animal ABC's*. As a result, she became familiar with the letters of the alphabet, and she would often put one letter on each of her pictures, imitating the book and perhaps her mother, Becky, who did a lot of writing. Becky noticed Adi's interest and after a while suggested, as teachers often do, that Adi might label her drawings. "You could put a name on that picture," she would say, "so people will know what it is." When Adi asked how to spell the word, Becky would say, "How does it sound to you?" On one occasion, Becky suggested that Adi might put little labels on her dresser drawers to help her remember where things went.

Becky and her husband, John, wanted to avoid pushing Adi, so they let her interests and enthusiasm guide them. If she had balked at the suggestion of labeling a picture, for example, they would have dropped the idea and waited awhile. But she had already shown an interest in writing by putting single letters on her own pictures, and she responded eagerly to their suggestion. "She liked writing, and it was something we could do together," Becky says.

Before long, Adi was labeling pictures on her own and putting up signs around the house such as "WET PAINT," "KEEP OUT," and "NO MEN ULUWD." Becky made little message boxes for everyone in the family, and Adi exchanged notes with her parents. As time went by, Adi's writing improved with very little direction from her mother. When she got to the point where she could write sentences, the two of them would sometimes write stories together. "I'll write a page, if you'll write a page," Becky would say.

When Adi was four-and-a-half, she began to read in much the same way as she had begun to write. Her parents had read to her regularly from infancy on. Every night, John would read to her for half an hour to an hour. Since Adi loved books and knew her letter sounds from writing, Becky began to play around a little with words in the books she read aloud. She would often point to each word as she read. In a book with a rhyme scheme, she would stop reading at the end of a line so that Adi could fill in the rhyming word. After a while, Becky tried it with nonrhyming words, just to see what Adi could do. Other times, Becky would read a line and then point to a word and ask, "Can you tell me what that word spells?"

These occasions were relatively rare; mostly the Rules read aloud just for fun. Becky wasn't expecting, or urging, Adi to start reading yet. They were just playing with words. But before long, Adi was trying to read on her own, and succeeding. She offered to read to household guests. She read road signs in the car, and she caught her mother if she skipped words in the books she read aloud. When the book was fairly simple, Becky could now say, "I'll read a page if you'll read a page," and they would read together.

By the time she turned five, Adi was writing and reading well—almost as if by magic, it seemed to her parents. They hadn't really done very much (much less than most teachers do in their efforts to get children to read and write in school). But even though it seemed that they had done little, the Rules had done a few very important things. They had demonstrated their own interest in writing and love of reading. They had made reading and writing part of their daily lives, a special and playful part of the time they spent with Adi. They had read enjoyable children's books, which, unlike basal readers, often have the rhymes and predictable patterns that help children start identifying words with ease. And they had provided Adi with opportunities for trying to read and write on her own, always watching to make sure she was enjoying the activities.

There would be a real danger if this method were used as a way to help your children get ahead earlier or sooner than other kids in the neighborhood. There's an enormous push in this country to make kids sprint ahead on skills. Too often, the reason for writing, or doing other activities, is entirely lost.

Adi Rule is not an average child (partly because of the way her parents have raised her). And no two children are alike in the steps they take and the pace they maintain on their way to literacy. So parents should not take her experience as any kind of timetable to be followed by their own children. Nevertheless, children are capable of doing much more than adults have realized. Many children in kindergarten write voluminously when given the chance. Aside from the speed with which she progressed, Adi had done the same things teachers have seen thousands of other children do—children of all abilities and backgrounds. Even for the Rule family, speed wasn't the point anyway; Adi's interests and enjoyment were. So parents can help their children develop a love for reading and writing if they, like the Rules, provide opportunities without pushing and then watch the child's reaction closely.

Raising a family, like writing or teaching, is a craft. You try a lot of different things. You have an inkling of something that might work, so you try it and then observe. After trying an experiment, you must have the confidence to abandon it or extend it further. If it doesn't work, you ask yourself, "What would be a better way to do that?"

Perhaps the easiest way to give children the chance to try writing is by making the necessary supplies available. Special-education teacher Susan Stires says, "Make sure that children have all the tools for writing, accessible and not necessarily put away. The more they trip over them, the more they are inclined to use them." She keeps pencils, crayons, and paper with her children's toys.

When young children write at home, they begin with labels, signs, notes, and lists, rather than full-fledged stories. Parents can make suggestions, but children with access to pencil and paper often come up with their own ideas. Stires's two daughters write as part of their play. "My children have always played waitress," she says. "They use writing. They make lists. As a matter of fact, Anne had a friend over today, and she was saying, 'When Amy gets here, we're going to play with the rabbits and swing and watch TV.' Then she said, 'I know! I'll make a list.' " Anne made a list, which showed not only how much writing was a part of her everyday life, but also how far one inventive speller had progressed by the end of first grade. In her list, which follows, she had to approximate the spelling of only one word.

Anne's and Amy's List.   12:00 to 3:30

Help my father.

My father will give us a big swing!

change   go swimming.

Play in campire (camper)

Have rabbits out

Watch TV.

read riddles

read jokes

Play

DONE!

Joan Tornow keeps a blackboard in each of her two sons' bedrooms. They like to make lists of their plans for the next day, even plans for playing with certain toys. Her sons use writing when they play, too. One day, a sign appeared on an alligator constructed out of blocks in the living room. "Do not feed the alligator," said one side of the sign. At the appropriate time, it could be flipped to the other side, which said, "Please feed the alligator."

Opportunities to write need not be restricted to playtime. In fact, researchers Jerome Harste, Caroline Burke, and Virginia Woodward have found that children who are constantly "dragged around" on errands and included in everyday chores and activities have an advantage over other children in learning to read and write. In their book *Language Stories and Literacy Lessons*, the researchers explain that the children they found to be at an advantage were the ones "who were reported as always 'under foot,' who naturally got included in cooking and setting the table, who were reported as writing out shopping lists and reading them during shopping, who were given paper and pen to write a letter to grandmother while a parent wrote letters or sent bills, who were given the occupant mail to open and read while the mother opened and read the rest of the mail."

Harste, Burke, and Woodward point out that parents often include children in such activities for practical rather than educational reasons. On the other hand, several researchers have found that those occasions when parents deliberately set out to instruct their children with workbooks or formal lessons often fall flat. Parents who understand the process by which children naturally learn to read and write avoid imitation school lessons. They are also more likely to appreciate their children's efforts at every stage. They may realize, for example, that the activity often referred to as "just scribbling" can reveal a child's budding knowledge of the written word. Harste, Burke, and Woodward compare scribbling from an American child, an Israeli child, and a Saudi Arabian child. The samples look as different as English, Hebrew, and Arabic writing, showing how much an advanced scribbler has already learned about the features of written language. In fact, when the Saudi Arabian four-year-old handed over her mock writing, she said, "Here, but you can't read it, 'cause I wrote it in Arabic and in Arabic we use a lot more dots than you do in English."

When Tornow's older son was in kindergarten, he surprised her with a note he wrote in invented spelling to a friend who had visited. At the time, Tornow was mildly amused. "If I had known what this was all about," she explains, "I would have been paying attention. I didn't see it [the note] as the germ of a larger thing. You get the impression that they're trying to write and that obviously they're not old enough, so you discount it."

Later, when she took a course on teaching writing, just to satisfy her own interest, she realized that she had not understood the importance of that note. "There are so many things children do that are landmarks or part of a progression," she says, "and if you know that, it is more exciting. When a child takes his first step, you know that he's going to run, or when he loses a tooth, you know he's going to get another tooth. You usually have some idea of what this is all leading to, but with writing, most of us don't."

With her new perspective, she found invented spelling charming. "There is something very endearing and cute about the way they spell these things, and I don't see what's wrong with enjoying the cuteness of that the same way you would enjoy it if a baby said *baw-baw* for bottle. I mean, here's *Thanksgiving,"* she says, flipping through a folder of her son's writing, *"T-a-c-s-g-v-a-e-g."*

RESPONDING TO CHILDREN

Once children do take the opportunity to read and write, parents often wonder how to respond to those efforts. Whether the topic under discussion is something the child has read, watched on TV, done, or written, parents can apply the same principle. Their role is to help children become aware of the knowledge they already possess. If the time seems to be right, parents can then use questions or suggestions to nudge children toward the next logical step in pursuit of their own interests. For parents of young children, the first question about when to nudge arises as the child begins using invented spelling.

When it comes to helping invented spellers, parents usually have neither experience nor training to draw on. It's hard for teachers, much less parents, to understand the sequences of growth children go through and to know what will help at different points. But someone who isn't acquainted with teaching procedures can never go wrong with letting learners know what they do well.

In *Understanding Writing,* edited by Thomas Newkirk and Nancie Atwell, Atkinson researcher Susan Sowers points out that children will make progress in invented spelling up to a certain point without any instruction at all. Beyond that point, she notes, teachers need to intervene to help children, and her article gives them suggestions on how to do that. Parents of preschool children, however, need not worry. Like Adi Rule, their children will be able to make rapid progress without much interference. Adi, for example, strung all her words together in one line when she began writing. Her parents never told her she was wrong or even talked about putting spaces between words. She did see conventional writing in books and her parents' notes, and on her own she picked up the idea that each word is a separate entity. First she used hyphens to mark the separations, and eventually she switched to the conventional spaces.

Let's say a little boy wants to write the word monster but doesn't know where to begin. I ask whether he can hear the first sound. If he knows the letter from games or reading we've done together, I say, "Put it down." If he doesn't, I may not teach the sound at that point because I still want the child to do more fooling around. He's making marks on paper, and those marks are wonderful. I'm in no hurry. If the child is demanding it, that's another story.

If the child does know the first sound, then I may try the last sound. Beginnings and endings are easy to get. Next I try the middle sound, all the while exclaiming over what the child already knows.

If he first writes the word MSTR (monster) on his own, I show him that I can read the word. "It says monster. You know why?" Then I make the sounds of M-S-T-R. Depending on the child's readiness and eagerness to go further, I may get into some of the vowels. Let's say he omits the n. (The nasal is often missed.) I have him say the word monster. If he doesn't put in an n sound when he says it slowly, then I have a pronunciation or discrimination problem.

Above all, the principle that I am working on here is letting the child know what he can do. In this instance, he knew M-S-T-R. That's a simple way of working. Later, if monster appears quite a bit in his writing I'll give him the full spelling of the word, underlining in red those letters that he already knows and possibly underlining in green the new ones to get.

Many parents are stumped when a child starts asking them questions. If the little boy writes MSTR and says, "Is that spelled right?" I ask another question: "Why did

you want to know?" It's just like a sex-education lesson;
you answer according to what the child wants. If he says,
"I just want to spell it right," I say, "Who is going to
read this?" If he says, "My mommy," or "Just me,"
then I say, "Well, you're thinking your mommy can't
read what you wrote?" It's all relative, depending on the
age. If the child is young, I want him to have enough
confidence in his own spelling to keep trying.

As they grow older, inventive spellers become aware that
their spelling is different from that in published books. But
thanks to good teaching or just the self-centeredness of childhood, they don't feel bad about it. Ellen Blackburn says her
first-graders accept that they still have much to learn, in
spelling as in everything else. Parents must be very careful
about giving young children the idea that their own spellings
are "wrong" or "bad." If children don't have confidence in
their own ability to try to spell a word, they'll give up trying.
And parents of children of any age do need to worry about
destroying self-confidence.

Parents often run amok when criticizing something a child
has written or said. Whether responding to a child's writing or
a dinner-table conversation, some parents leave the impression that the child can do nothing right. One mother is well
aware of the stifling effect of excessive parental criticism.
"My father was a perfectionist," she recalls, "and at the
dinner table we were not allowed to say, 'I feel pretty good,'
because *pretty* was an adjective describing how something
appeals to your eye. Therefore, you cannot feel 'pretty good.'
With this every-night carping, our dinner table became very
quiet. We used to talk abut how free Wednesday nights were,
when Dad had Lions' Club meetings. We could tell jokes, and
we could sit with our elbows on the table." After volunteering
to help out in an Atkinson classroom where children wrote
freely, she began to see the connections between stifling
criticism at the dinner table and in the classroom.

The mother had some insights into the cause of her own
father's behavior. After growing up on a farm, he had gone to
Harvard University and eventually became a highly success-

ful business executive. In the process he turned into "pretty much of a snob" as he worked hard to advance himself socially, and it was in fear of any "possible relapse" that he maintained such rigid standards of speech. Fear is often the motivating force behind excessive parental criticism. At best, parental fears may simply have a chilling effect, as the children at the executive's family dinner table discovered. At worst, those fears can turn into self-fulfilling prophecy.

> *Parents who believe that they themselves were poor learners are afraid their children will be. A classic example is a parent who has had a reading problem and becomes all upset when a child stumbles on one word. He may have read the first three correctly and missed the fourth, but his parent says, "Oh my God, he's just like me!" Another parent whose child made the same error might say, "Look at that! She's almost there!"*
>
> *In working with writing, the parents' chief role is to let their child know what they understand and what they have learned from the piece. If there are parts that confuse the parent, then the parent should ask plain, honest questions that give the child the responsibility of explaining what the reader needs to know. If a paper is messy, uses confusing language, or is illegible, then the parent says, "I can't figure this out. Help me."*

In short many parents do more harm than good because they feel compelled to behave like an old-fashioned schoolteacher. Both parents and teachers can be of more help by responding as honest readers. First, they can show their interest, and priorities, by responding to the content of a piece of writing. Then by asking for the writer's help, readers can show where more work is needed in the piece, without shaming the writer. Notice the difference in tone between different ways of phrasing the same comment. "This sentence confused me" has quite a different effect from "This sentence is confusing" or, worse, "This sentence is a mess." A statement like "This handwriting is atrocious" condemns the writer. "I can't make this out," on the other hand, demonstrates the true purpose for legible writing. Parents, like teachers, can also help by focusing on one problem at a time. Writers can't attend to all their errors at once, anyway, and if they are forced to try, they're not likely to want to keep writing.

Finally, parents should beware of coming down hard on a child who appears to be regressing, in writing or any other skill. Often it is best to wait and see what happens next. Many an apparent regression has turned out to be just a minor setback on the way to a major breakthrough. It is only natural to grasp the gist of a new concept or rule before learning its refinements and exceptions. A three-year-old who has just discovered that an -*ed* ending puts a verb into the past tense may say *breaked* for *broke*. When Adi Rule first discovered a silent *e,* she began attaching *e*s to the end of her words willy-nilly. Even an adult who has just learned that a compound adjective is hyphenated before a noun may write "scantily-clad teenager," unaware that phrases including an adverb ending in -*ly* do not require the hyphen. Thus, an error is often actually a sign of progress.

On the other hand, praise can cause problems, as well. I am not saying that praise should not be given. But praise is often used as a substitute for thinking. And if compliments are given indiscriminately, they simply aren't heard when they really are merited. Praise can also be used to manipulate because it makes the receiver overly beholden to the giver.

Instead of telling a child "That was very good," I could say, "I notice that when you wrote about the boy and his dog, you showed how the boy would lean down, hug the dog, and nuzzle him. And because of the way you described his face when he did it, I understood how much the dog meant to him." Better still, I might quote the phrase or line I'm referring to. In this case, I don't have to tell the child this is good writing. I have shown that it is with my specific example. Thus, the writer knows that I cared enough to select the details to give to her as a kind of gift. Good teaching gives the gift of attention in such a way that children are able to give themselves gifts when the teacher is no longer present.

Praise can be insulting when it implies that the receivers couldn't figure out for themselves what's good or bad. In the example of the piece about the boy and the dog, the writer will now be able to recognize on her own when her writing is good and therefore be able to give herself a gift of self-praise when the adult isn't there. This approach encourages independence. Unfortunately, in most classrooms or homes, children are constantly seeking out an adult for praise as if they themselves could never tell whether something is good—or as if only an adult's approval could make it good.

The occasional well-timed question also nudges children a little further in the direction of independence. Good questions challenge children to think, and eventually to think about thinking—that is, to learn how to learn. When it comes to talking about things children have read, written, or even watched on TV, teachers recommend asking genuine, open-ended questions. The parent must want to know what the child has to say. Children can sense when an adult has an answer ready in advance. Many good questions begin with *why:* "Why do you think the person did that?" a parent might ask about a character in a book or TV show.

Ask questions that get children to evaluate and speculate. When a child has read, seen, or written a story, ask the child's opinion about favorite parts and characters. Together, talk about what you think might happen next in the story, based on what has already occurred.

One type of question parents may not be familiar with is the *process question,* which focuses children's attention on what they have done or will do in the process of reading and writing: How many drafts did you go through? How did you choose this topic? What's going to happen next? Was this hard for you to read? How did you figure that out? These questions help children start thinking about thinking.

Of course, process questions need not be restricted to discussions of writing. To me, it's not writing as much as a way of viewing how people learn. In math, if a child gets something right, I say, "That's right. How did you figure that out?" Then children will soon start to ask themselves, "How did I do that?" We're usually saying, "That's wrong. Why did you do that?" That's no fun.

Sometimes the best question gives back to the child responsibility for choosing the next step. I ask, "And what do you need to learn next? What do you need help with now?" I may think I know what the child needs, but I always try to treat children with respect. I ask questions based on the assumption that they want to learn. Too many directives and questions are based on the assumption that children do not want to learn. After a healthy dose of that, our worst fears are confirmed: children fight learning. It's the same thing with lies. Tell children they're liars, and the odds are that the next time they will lie.

Parents can safely assume that children do want to learn. When their work or play receives a warm response and a few well-timed questions and suggestions, children find their own ways to challenge themselves. Adi Rule surprised her mother often with her ability to tackle new projects. One day shortly before she turned five, Adi disappeared into the study to do some writing. After a while, Becky went in to see what she was doing. Adi had written this:

NASHNAL-NOOS-PAPR	National Newspaper
THISWEKAND	This weekend
ATTHERRULE	at the Rules'
BABDUCK	baby ducks
GRODBIGR	growed bigger.

Becky was thrilled. She and John read the newspaper every night and Adi enjoyed the comics. Sometimes her parents pointed out pictures of animals or other things that might interest her. But she had come up with the idea of doing her own newspaper all by herself. And her attempt revealed that she had a clear grasp of the purpose and even, to some extent, the format of newspapers. The word *National* was somewhat of a mystery, but Becky guessed that it had come from *National Geographic,* Adi's favorite magazine.

After exclaiming with delight at what Adi had done, Becky asked her one question: "What else happened?" When Becky returned, Adi had added a second news item:

OSOTHISWKAND	Also this weekend
THE RULESWENT	the Rules went
TOHRMIT	to Hermit
ILEND	Island

Becky again expressed her pleasure and asked once more, "What else happened?" When she returned to the study, Adi had added her name and a final message at the bottom of the page: REDMORTMORO (read more tomorrow).

Adi, too, was pleased with her newspaper. She read it aloud to herself several times, reading *grew* instead of *growed* on the second and third readings. Aware that newspapers come out in many copies, she decided to make her own "copies" on her mother's typewriter. She knew how to replace the expensive single-strike ribbon with the multi-strike cartridge, but she had trouble putting in the paper, so she enlisted her mother's help. Then Adi typed her first "copy," which turned out to be a new draft of the original.

NASHNAL-NOOS-PAPR!	National Newspaper!
THISWKAND	This weekend
ATTHERULES	at the Rules
BABDUCKS	baby ducks
WRBORNOSOTHISWKANDTHE	were born. Also this weekend, the
RULESWENT!	Rules went
TO-HRMIT	to Hermit
ILEND	Island
REDMORTMORO	Read more tomorrow.
IMSOHAPE	I'm so happy
THATTIM	that I'm
GOING	going
TO-MA-KOPES	to make copies.
THEand	The end.
By-ADI	By Adi.

Although Adi had occasionally crossed out a letter here and there to change her spelling in the past, Becky was surprised at how much Adi had changed her first "copy." She had not only added punctuation and corrected some spelling, but she had also rewritten one whole sentence about the baby ducks. When asked why, Adi revealed a surprising sensitivity to the needs of "NOOS-PAPR" readers outside the family: "They didn't know the ducks were born yet," she explained. After Adi had made nine copies, many of which bore no resemblance to the original, Becky suggested that they go into town to make photocopies for friends and relatives.

CHAPTER TEN

FORMAL SCHOOLING FOR FOUR-YEAR-OLDS? NO.

by Edward Zigler

A developing momentum is moving our nation toward universal preschool education. Many decision-makers are currently advocating the downward extension of public schooling to four-year-olds. New York's Mayor Koch has not only made all-day kindergarten mandatory, but has appointed a commission charged with the creation of a public school program for all four-year-olds. A recent *New York Times* editorial entitled "School at 4: A Model for the Nation" hailed Koch's initiative as the most sensible way to "save the next generation." American Federation of Teachers president Albert Shanker has also endorsed preschool education.

So many positive voices have been heard that it is easy to assume that schooling for four-year-olds is an uncontested issue met only with popular support and enthusiasm. Indeed the Commissioner for Education in New York State, Gordon Ambach, stated that it was not possible to find anyone to

---

Should positive preschool experiences, like those of the Perry Preschool Project, be used as the basis for instituting universal early education throughout the country? Are parents and teachers rushing children into reading and writing and sacrificing some of the precious social aspects of growing up? In this chapter, Professor Edward Zigler—one of the founders of Head Start—considers these questions. He proposes that there are better, less costly ways to give youngsters a good start.

uphold the negative side of the issue. However, there are some negative voices, and they are beginning to be heard. Herbert Zimiles, a leading thinker in the field of early childhood education, recently argued that the movement toward universal preschool education is characterized more by enthusiasm than by thought. The Commissioner of Education for the State of Connecticut, Gerald Tirozzi (another champion of public education for four-year-olds) established a committee to study the issue within the general context of children's services. In their recommendations, this committee concluded that "under no circumstances do we believe it appropriate for all four-year-olds to be involved in a 'kindergarten-type' program within the public schools." I now add my voice to those who have argued that universal schooling for four-year-olds requires more thought than has been accorded this issue.

The current impetus for earlier schooling has two sources. The first is the concern generated by the recent proliferation of negative evaluations of our public secondary schools. The National Commission on Excellence in Education report, *A Nation at Risk* (1983), detailed the failures of secondary schooling in America. Similar studies soon followed. These reports emphasized the need for higher academic standards, more attention to basics, more rigor in teaching, and longer school days and years. Few of them proposed earlier schooling as a solution to our educational problems.

An ostensible exception to this, Mortimer Adler's thoughtful *Paideia Proposal* (1983), did link school reform and early childhood education. Adler stated: "Preschool deprivation is the cause of backwardness or failure in school . . . hence at least one year—or better, two or three years of preschool tutelage must be provided for those who do not get such preparation from favorable environments." Too often, however, Adler's caveat with regard to the purely remedial nature of preschool for the disadvantaged is ignored. It is not Adler's opinion, nor is it mine, that the more advantaged children in our society require compulsory preschool education at public's expense.

A second source of the momentum toward universal preschool education is the inappropriate generalization of the effects of some excellent early intervention programs. Several preschool intervention programs such as Head Start, the New York University Institute for Developmental Studies, the Ypsilanti-based Perry Preschool Program, the New York State pre-kindergarten program, the Brookline Early Education Program, have succeeded in spurring the developmental and cognitive growth of economically disadvantaged three- and four-year-old children. But extrapolation to all children from these programs is inappropriate for two reasons. First, benefits were obtained only for economically disadvantaged children. Second, these intervention programs differ from standard school fare in a number of important ways. Unlike conventional schoolings, these interventions are provided to the family as a whole, not simply to a target child; a vital difference, as many theorists believe that preschool programs are most successful when parents participate and the programs share a commitment to the non-educational needs of the children and families they serve, including health-oriented and social services.

Public preschool education shares few of these services and concerns, nor can they become the primary focus of the educational establishment. It is an open question whether early school-based programs will result in the same benefits— benefits which may well be a consequence of services having very little to do with formal education. It was precisely those differences between Head Start and formal schooling which I have outlined here that led many of us to oppose President Carter's proposal to move Head Start into the new Department of Education, and that in the end prevented its inclusion.

THE PERRY PRESCHOOL PROGRAM

Additional differences must be considered when interpreting the benefits of the Perry Preschool Program. This well-known exemplary intervention effort which achieved remarkable success is deserving of the praise it has received from many quarters. It is one of the few intervention efforts that attempted to assign participants to experimental and control groups. Further, it is one of the even smaller number of intervention efforts that meet the demand that the assessment of early intervention efforts include a cost-benefit analysis.

However, generalization to typical public programs is highly problematic for three reasons. First, it is very unlikely that a preschool program mounted in the typical public school will be of the quality represented by the Perry Preschool Project. The program's experimental character ensured that it would be exceptionally well planned, monitored, and managed. Further, participating in an experiment can stimulate and motivate the staff. Researchers worked extensively with direct child caregivers in analyzing and constructing the program, visiting experts held weekly seminars for the entire preschool staff. While the consequences of these aspects of the program were not analyzed, their potential effect on the outcome may well have been substantial.

Second, the Perry sample was not only nonrepresentative of children in general; there is some question whether it was representative of even the bulk of economically disadvantaged children. The sample was limited to black children, when in fact the majority of low-income children are white; it is even problematic as to whether the sample is representative of low-income black children. The Perry Project was limited to children with IQ's between 61 and 88. Yet, the median IQ of black children in the U.S. was 80-85 in the early 1960's.

A further argument against generalization from the Perry Preschool Project derives from the fact that participation was fully voluntary and thus introduces a self-selection phenomenon (how families that did not choose to volunteer differed from the final project sample is an open question).

Finally, the Perry Project poses a number of methodological difficulties. First, to be in the intervention group, the child had to have a parent at home during the day, resulting in a significant difference between control and intervention groups on maternal employment. Second, primary data collectors were community people who had close and supportive ties with the families.

Third, assignment to experimental and control groups was

not totally random, resulting in problems of interpretation. Finally, criticisms have been advanced that the Perry programs cost-benefit analyses overestimates the benefits attributed to the intervention.

Caution should be exercised in generalizing from one population to another. I would like to see the outcome of the High/ Scope model when mounted by people with less expertise than those employed in the Perry Project. Furthermore, evaluations of any intervention should be conducted by researchers not involved in the development of the model being evaluated. Given the pervasiveness of self-fulfilling prophecies, this caveat represents merely a common-sense concern.

APPROPRIATE CANDIDATES FOR INTERVENTION

The High/Scope data generate the intriguing hypothesis that preschool intervention is particularly effective for the most economically disadvantaged children, a view supported by the New York State evaluation of its experimental preschool program. The New York study indicated that the only cognitive gains that lasted beyond the preschool period were among children whose mothers were of the lowest educational index.

This view has apparently not escaped educational decision-makers. Almost all the states that now provide school-sponsored programs for four-year-olds limit enrollment to low-income, handicapped and, in some cases, non-English-speaking youngsters. Even the Ypsilanti group recognizes that these are the children who can profit most from intervention. In any case, the results for children of educated parents were far less pronounced than for the children of less educated parents, and such differences as were found may have been short-term, as no long-term assessment has been carried out. In contrast, there is a large body of evidence that indicates that there is little, if anything, to be gained by exposing middle-class children to early education.

American schools are already under great financial pressure and must make the most efficient use possible of limited economic resources. I have long been an advocate of cost-benefit analyses for all types of social programs. As previously stated, our best thinking suggests we can make the most effective use of limited funds by investing them in intervention programs that target three overlapping groups: (1) the economically disadvantaged child, (2) the handicapped and (3) the bilingual. Spreading education budgets to all four-year-olds would spread them too thin. Such an extension would not only have little effect on the more advantaged mainstream, but would diminish our capacity to intervene with those who could benefit the most.

There is, however, one potential advantage to universal preschool education. A weakness of Head Start and Head Start-like programs is their built-in economic segregation of children. Poor children go to Head Start, while more affluent children go elsewhere. Universal preschool would better integrate children across socioeconomic lines and would introduce equity into early childhood programs. While this would provide preschool education to children who do not need it, it would guarantee its availability to children who do. Yet, while we would be well-advised to promote the integration of children from diverse social and ethnic backgrounds, the cost of doing so through universal preschool education outweigh potential benefits.

THE REAL PROBLEM

Educators in several states point to the pressure for all-day kindergarten as evidence of the value parents place on early education, but I believe they have misread this demand. What many parents are expressing is less a burning desire for preschool education than their need for quality day care. Fifty-nine percent of the mothers of three- and four-year-olds, are now employed outside their homes, many of whom enroll their children in child-care programs that provide organized educational activities. Ironically, not even all-day kindergarten programs are able to fill adequately the day-care needs of families with both parents working outside the home. Schools tend to adjourn around 3:00, two hours before most working days end. The day-care problem has only been moved back for a few hours, and this token improvement may actually lead parents to take fewer precautions for those relatively few hours.

Day care can be prohibitively expensive for many families, and it is not surprising that many would prefer to shift the cost to the public school system. The Perry Preschool Project was estimated by its originators to cost approximately $1,500 per year per child in 1963. Given the number of three- and four-year-olds in the nation today, and adjusting these figures for inflation, the total cost of a universal child-development program would be many billions of dollars per year. Unfortunately, advocates of universal preschool education continue to behave as though these vast sums will magically appear. Fiscal reality demands we target populations who can most benefit from care, and provide programs best suited to their particular needs.

We must also listen to those families who neither need nor want their young children placed in preschool programs. The compulsory aspect of many of the proposed early education plans has angered many parents and set them in opposition to school officials—a poor beginning to the positive home-school relationship which is vital to the educational process. Decision-makers must be sensitive to the individual needs of children and parents; they should recognize that, whenever the family situation permits it, the best place for a preschool child is at home. We must strive to be sensitive to the individual differences between young children. Some four-year-olds can handle a five or six hour school day; many others cannot. Whenever it is best for the child to be at home with the parents, we should try to make it possible for him or her to be at home. This is not to ignore the fact that home may be a place of abuse or neglect, a welfare hotel, or a confusing and insecure environment lacking adequate resources. For these children, day care may be the best alternative.

Yet, many competent, caring parents who are at home resent school administrators' proposals to keep the preschool child in a full-day early education program. Staying at home is an option for these families, and compulsory education would needlessly deprive parents and children of valuable time they could spend together. In fact, conversations children carry on at home may be the richest source of linguistic and cognitive enrichment for children of all economic levels. The fact that parent and child share a common life and frame of reference allow them to explore events and ideas in intimate, individualistic conversations with great personal meaning.

A TIME FOR CHILDHOOD

We are driving our young children too hard, and thereby deprive them of their most precious commodity—their childhood. The image of the four-year-old in designer jeans with a miniature executive briefcase may seem cute, but going from cradle to school denies children the freedom to develop at their own pace. Children are growing up too fast today, and prematurely placing four-year-olds and five-year-olds into full-day preschool education programs will only compound this problem.

Those who argue in favor of universal preschool education ignore evidence which indicates that early schooling is inappropriate for many four-year-olds, and may even be harmful to their development. Marie Winn (1983) notes in *Children Without Childhood* that premature schooling can replace valuable play time, slowing or reducing the child's overall development. This is especially true with the present cognitive thrust, where there is danger of overemphasizing formal and overly structured academics. The care of very young children must be a distinct form of care suited to the rapid developmental changes and high dependency of these children, not a scaled-down version of a grade-school curriculum. At the same time, we must remember that, while early childhood is an important and sensitive period, it is not uniquely so. In the 1960s we believed early childhood was a magic period during which minimal intervention efforts would have maximal, indelible effects on the child. In the current push toward early formal education we can see the unfortunate recurrence of this idea.

Every age of the child is a magic period. We must be just as concerned for the six-year-old, the ten-year-old, and the sixteen-year-old as we are for the four-year-old. In fact, the proposed New York plan is especially troubling in that it includes a suggestion to add a year of education at the beginning of formal schooling and to drop a year at the end of high school. We must guard against shortchanging one age group in our efforts to help another.

THE EASY WAY OUT

This is not the first time universal preschool education has been proposed. Wilson Riles, then California State Superintendent of Schools, advocated early childhood education ten years ago just as school superintendents in New York and Connecticut do today. Then as now, the arguments in favor of preschool education were that it would reduce school failure, lower drop-out rates, increase test scores and produce a generation of more competent high school graduates.

My interpretation of the evidence, the same as that finally reached by the State of California, is that preschool education will achieve none of these results. I am not simply saying that universal preschool education will be a waste of time and money. There is a danger in asserting that the solution to poor performance in school, and later in life, by the disadvantaged will be solved by a year of preschool education. The nation is on the verge of falling into the overoptimistic trap that ensnared us in the mid-sixties, when expectations were raised that an eight-week summer program could solve all the problems of the poor. If we wish to improve the lives of the economically disadvantaged we must abandon the inoculation models of the sixties and work for much deeper social reforms. The tokenistic nature of relying on educational innovations alone to solve the problems of poor children has been noted by historian Marvin Lazerson:

*Too often discussions of educational reform appear to be
a means of avoiding more complex and politically dan-*

gerous issues . . . education is . . . cheaper than new housing and new jobs. We are left with greater school responsibility while the social problems which have the greatest effect on schooling are largely ignored. The schools—in this case, preschool—are asked to do too much, and given too little support to accomplish what they are asked. A variety of interest groups, however, are satisfied: educators, because they get status and funds, social reformers, because they believe in education, and government officials because they pass positive legislation without upsetting traditional social patterns.

We simply cannot inoculate children in one year against the ravages of a life of deprivation. Even champions of early childhood education have made sobering statements warning us not to expect too much while doing too little. Fred Hechinger wrote "Part of the problem is to overpromise and under finance. The hard fact is: there are no educational miracles against the effects of poverty." In an incisive analysis, Senator Daniel Patrick Moynihan agrees, warning that exaggerated reports of success in the field of early childhood education lead inevitably to near nihilism when these extravagant hopes are unfulfilled: "From finding out that not everything works, we rush to the judgment that nothing works or can be made to work." Moynihan notes the Ypsilanti researchers were restrained in their claims of the benefits of early childhood education, stating that such programs are "part of the solution, not the whole solution."

A REALISTIC SOLUTION

Educators must realize that they cannot reform the world or change the basic nature of children. The real question is how to provide the best experience during the day for four-year-olds, specifically for those who cannot remain at home with a consistent, competent caregiver. Parents do not need children who read at age four, but they do need affordable, high-quality child care. The most cost-effective way to provide universally available—again, not compulsory—care would be to work from the school. Yes, I am advocating a return to the concept of the community school, oriented towards the needs of the family and neighborhood, which could provide full-day, high-quality child care for four- and even three-year-old children in school buildings already present in the community. Although such programs would include a developmentally appropriate educational component, they would primarily be places for recreation and socialization—the real business of preschoolers. In-school day care could also easily accommodate older children after school is dismissed.

Such a program, although operating on school grounds, should not be staffed solely by teachers. Instead, I propose staffing school-based day-care programs with teachers in a supervisory capacity, and Child Development Associates, certified child care persons, currently used in Head Start programs. Certification of CDAs is based not on educational attainment alone, but on proven competence in meeting all the needs of children. I would champion the whole child approach best exemplified in Barbara Biber's Bank Street model. New York University's educational enrichment program of the Institute for Developmental Studies is another excellent example of a program using a sound whole child approach. On a larger scale, many aspects of funding will have to be addressed, such as tax base and licensing procedures. Federal support might be expected to subsidize costs for economically disadvantaged children. Money would also be saved by making use of existing school facilities.

Finally, in thinking of three- and four-year-olds, let us not neglect the needs of five-year-olds. I believe that a full day of formal schooling is too much even for these children. Instead, I would propose a half-day kindergarten program to be followed by a half day in school day care for those who need it. The extra cost could be borne by parents on a sliding scale, with financial assistance available to needy families. Licensed qualified teachers would teach a half day in the morning and certified CDAs would care for the children in the afternoon. A half day of education is plenty for a five-year old.

Again, let me emphasize that the day-care element should be strictly voluntary; no parent who wants his or her child at home after school should be denied this option.

In short, we must ask ourselves, what would we be buying for our children in universal preschool education programs, and at what cost? The family-oriented, multi-service community school could meet the varied needs of preschoolers and their families with a cafeteria of programs from which families could select what suits them best. Such services could include comprehensive intervention programs, health and nutrition components, high quality, affordable day care, and educational opportunities, to name only a few possibilities. Our four-year-olds do have a place in school, but it is not in a classroom.

CHAPTER ELEVEN

GOOD DAY CARE— A NATIONAL NEED

by Tony Schwartz

The other day, I had a long conversation with Susan Weissman, the director of the day-care center that my four-year-old daughter has attended since she was six months old. For the past several years, Susan has run three private not-for-profit day-care centers in Manhattan. Each year, she has lost money, and each year she has made up the difference herself. She is a woman who is deeply committed to day care, energetic and usually buoyant. But when we spoke recently, Susan could not hide her despair about the future of day care.

In cities around the country—from Washington to Des Moines to San Francisco—the demand for day care far outstrips the available spaces. The Ad Hoc Day Care Coalition recently characterized the unmet need for adequate child care as a crisis. Nearly two-thirds of all mothers with children less than three years old are now working. The number of mothers returning to work within a year of childbirth has virtually doubled since 1970.

The simple truth is that it is extremely difficult to operate a self-supporting high-quality facility without charging rates so high that most families cannot possibly afford them. And while there is some public support for parents at the lowest

---

The quality of day care is an issue that concerns parents and day-care centers alike. How do centers catering to two-job, middle-class parents, with no public funding, provide good care and pay their bills? In this article, from the January 3, 1986, issue of The New York Times, *the scope of the dilemma is pondered by a journalist and father of a preschooler.*

end of the income scale, there's not nearly enough to make quality care available to all working parents.

Rent, particularly in a city like New York, is one of the prohibitive costs. But infants also require considerable supervision and attention; the child-teacher ratio at Park Center, which our daughter attends, is three or four to one. Many day-care centers keep costs low by paying employees minimum wage or just slightly more. But you get what you pay for. Low-paid caretakers often have minimal qualifications, and turnover rates are high.

Susan, who charges parents higher rates than do public centers, can pay her teachers better salaries. But to keep the best of them, she must reward them with raises, and even at that she can't match the salaries being paid to first year public school teachers. Against that backdrop, Susan is being forced to close one of her own centers this month—victim of yet another luxury development.

All of this makes me despair, too. Day care is one of the best things that ever happened to my wife and me. Kate, our older daughter, has flourished at Park Center, and we hope to send our six-month-old, Emily, to Park Center next year.

When Kate was born, my wife took a six-month maternity leave from her full-time job. During that period, we debated about what sort of care would be best for Kate when Deborah returned to work. Most of our professional friends with young children had housekeepers and insisted that infants require one-to-one care. But we'd also heard horror stories about the difficulty of finding—and keeping—quality caretakers, and so we decided to visit several local day-care centers.

To our surprise, we were immediately captivated by the intelligence and warmth of the teachers and by the enthusiasm and liveliness of the children. It was no small bonus that day care totally solved the problem of reliability.

Kate had just learned to sit when she spent her first full day at Park Center. She did not cry when we left her (although we did), and in the four years since then, I can count on my hands the number of days she's been reluctant to go to school in the morning.

At Park Center, she has developed something akin to an

extended family, which includes the other children, many of whom she's shared a classroom with for three years, the parents and, perhaps above all, the teachers. Two teachers— Marlene Wilburn and Adela Eccles—have been with Kate since she began in day care.

When I ask Kate each evening what she did in school that day, she invariably answers, "Play, silly." I am delighted that she sees it that way. But I am also happy that in the course of playing, Kate has learned how to add and subtract, how to read and write a couple of dozen words and how to draw realistic human figures. Day care, in short, has been far more than a babysitting service for us.

The vast majority of working parents in America work primarily because they need the money. So long as that is true, any debate over whether it may be better for young children to have at least one parent at home full-time is academic. Nor can most working parents afford full-time one-to-one care.

Unfortunately, individuals like Susan Weissman are too few and far between. To survive and prosper, day care—affordable, high-quality and carefully regulated—must become a national priority. For corporations, there is an obvious self-interest in supporting and subsidizing day care services. Employees who can rest assured that their children are reliably and well cared for will be freed to work more productively. In addition, city, state and Federal governments should become more involved. The only industrialized nation that lacks a national policy on child care is the United States.

The bottom line, of course, is that our children are our future. We can only hope to get back from them as much as we put in. The first responsibility plainly is our own, as parents. But we must also create for our children nourishing and nurturing environments when we cannot be there. If we do not, we'll surely pay the price later.

Quality day care can be a wonderful option. Deborah and I—and Kate most of all—know from experience. Day care may not be appropriate for everyone. But at the very least, it should be one of the available choices in a society that now offers working parents far too few.

POSTSCRIPT

Fred M. Hechinger

A last word: I am convinced that the issue is not whether to move into early childhood education; the issue is how to move successfully.

At a time when budgets are strained, there is a great temptation to try to deal with young children on the cheap. Turning youngsters over to poorly qualified caretakers could do irreparable harm at worst; but even at best, it would fail to provide the kind of physical, emotional and intellectual nurturing ideally expected of warm and literate households. Since three- and four-year-olds cannot express their criticism of poorly run early childhood education programs, adults who are in charge and parents who use such programs must shoulder a very special responsibility to make sure that children are well served, not simply stored away.

In many communities, the concept of early childhood education is still a new and uncharted field. I have tried to select from the available experiences some of the best examples of what might be done. This is not intended to prescribe one best way to deal with youngsters; it is merely an attempt to open adult minds to the need and the options. I have tried to select, from a growing literature, some reports of successful programs, an indication of children's responses, suggestions of hazards to avoid, and hints for parents on how to join the experts in seeking to give children a better start. If I were to express one single concern that emerges from all these chapters and reinforces my own bias, it is that the children must be surrounded by adults who are both loving and understanding of the way children think. The idea is not to impose adult goals but rather to turn childhood into a time of joy, with constant encouragement of growth and development. If there is one theme that runs through all the chapters, it is that early childhood education should not be a pressure cooker. Unwarranted pressure is not the alternative to inacceptable neglect.

Sensible voices are being raised by highly qualified experts, such as Edward Zigler, warning against the creation of one more monolithic system. A good case can be made against one more universal requirement. Parents should be allowed as many choices as possible, including the choice not to participate at all. This clearly implies that there is nothing wrong with asking those who can afford it to pay for all or part of the services. And the wise and lively account of the joys and benefits of "Learning At Home" by Donald Graves and Virginia Stuart, and Mildred Winter's "Parents As First Teachers" are ample testimony of what can be accomplished at home, even if not in every home. In fact, there is much that teachers can also learn from those chapters. I repeat: There is no one best way.

No less essential, however, is a firm new commitment to make early childhood education freely available to all children of poverty as an investment in their, and society's, future. We have continued far too long to feed generation after generation of children into a pipeline to nowhere. We have raised too many children without allowing them expectations of success, without giving them hopes of useful lives ahead. To continue to do so, in an era that has no economic or social use for the uneducated, is to court disaster. The pioneering efforts cited in the preceding pages offer a new departure—costly at first but immensely profitable in the long run. It promises a better start for millions of children.

APPENDIX

PARENTS' GUIDE TO DAY CARE

The following list, recommended in Chapter 8, was prepared by the Department of Health and Human Services in 1980 (DHHS Publication No. (DHDS) 84-30270). It is a summary of the qualities that parents should look for in a day-care center—before enrolling their child.

DOES YOUR CHILD'S CAREGIVER . . .
(For All Children)

- Appear to be warm and friendly?
- Seem calm and gentle?
- Seem to have a sense of humor?
- Seem to be someone with whom you can develop a relaxed, sharing relationship?
- Seem to be someone your child will enjoy being with?
- Seem to feel good about herself and her job?
- Have child-rearing attitudes and methods that are similar to your own?
- Treat each child as a special person?
- Understand what children can and want to do at different stages of growth?
- Have the right materials and equipment on hand to help them learn and grow mentally and physically?
- Patiently help children solve their problems?
- Provide activities that encourage children to think things through?
- Encourage good health habits, such as washing hands before eating?
- Talk to the children and encourage them to express themselves through words and language?

- Encourage children to express themselves in creative ways?
- Have art and music supplies suited to the ages of all children in care?
- Seem to have enough time to look after all the children in her or his care?
- Help your child to know, accept, and feel good about him- or herself?
- Help your child become independent in ways you approve?
- Help your child learn to get along with and to respect other people, no matter what their backgrounds are?
- Provide a routine and rules the children can understand and follow?
- Accept and respect your family's cultural values?
- Take time to discuss your child with you regularly?
- Have previous experience or training in working with children?
- Have a yearly physical exam and TB test?

And if you have an infant or toddler (birth to age three)

- Seem to enjoy cuddling your baby?
- Care for your baby's physical needs such as feeding and diapering?
- Spend time holding, playing with, talking to your baby?
- Provide stimulation by pointing out things to look at, touch, and listen to?
- Provide dependable and consistent care so your baby can form an attachment and feel important?
- Cooperate with your efforts to toilet train your toddler?
- "Child-proof" the setting so your toddler can crawl or walk safely and freely.
- Realize that toddlers want to do things for themselves and help your child to learn to feed and dress him- or herself, go to the bathroom, and pick up his or her own toys?
- Help your child learn the language by talking with him or her, naming things, reading aloud, describing what she or he is doing, and responding to your child's words?

And if your child is a preschooler (age three to five or six)

- Plan many different activities for your child?
- Join in the children's activities?

- Set consistent limits which help your child gradually learn to make his or her own choices?
- Recognize the value of play and encourage your child to be creative and use his or her imagination?
- Help your child feel good about him- or herself by being attentive, patient, positive, warm, and accepting?
- Allow your child to do things for him- or herself because he/she understands children can learn from their mistakes?
- Help your child increase his or her vocabulary by talking with him or her, reading aloud, and answering questions?

DOES THE DAY-CARE HOME OR CENTER HAVE . . .
(For All Children)

- An up-to-date license, if one is required?
- A clean and comfortable look?
- Enough space indoors and out so all the children can move freely and safely?
- Enough caregivers to give attention to all of the children in care?
- Enough furniture, playthings, and other equipment for all the children in care?
- Equipment that is safe and in good repair?
- Equipment and materials that are suitable for the ages of the children in care?
- Enough room and cots or cribs so the children can take naps?
- Enough clean bathrooms for the children in care?
- Safety caps on electrical outlets?
- A safe place to store medicines, household cleaners, poisons, matches, sharp instruments, and other dangerous items?
- An alternate exit in case of fire?
- A safety plan to follow in emergencies?
- An outdoor play area that is safe, fenced, and free of litter?
- Enough heat, light, and ventilation?
- Nutritious meals and snacks made with the kinds of food you want your child to eat?
- A separate place to care for sick children where they can be watched?
- A first aid kit?
- Fire extinguishers?

- Smoke detectors?
- Covered radiators and protected heaters?
- Strong screens or bars on windows above the first floor?

And if you have an infant or toddler (birth to age three)

- Gates at tops and bottoms of stairs?
- A potty chair or special toilet seat in the bathroom?
- A clean and safe place to change diapers?
- Cribs with firm mattresses covered in heavy plastic?
- Separate crib sheets for each baby in care?

And if your child is a preschooler (aged three to five or six)

- A stepstool in the bathroom so your preschooler can reach the sink and toilet?

ARE THERE OPPORTUNITIES . . .
(For All Children)

- To play quietly and actively indoors and out?
- To play alone at times and with friends at other times?
- To follow a schedule that meets young children's need for routine but that is flexible enough to meet the needs of each child?
- To use materials and equipment that help children learn new physical skills and to control and exercise their muscles?
- To learn to get along, to share, and to respect themselves and others?
- To learn about their own and others' cultures through art, music, books, songs, games, and other activities?
- To speak both English and their family's native language?
- To watch special programs on television that have been approved by you?

And if you have an infant or toddler (brith to age three)

- To crawl and explore safely?
- To play with objects and toys that help infants to develop their senses of touch, sight, and hearing? (For example, mobiles, mirrors, cradle gyms, crib toys, rattles, things to squeeze and roll, pots and pans, nesting cups, different-sized boxes)
- To take part in a variety of activities that are suited to toddlers' short attention spans? (For example, puzzles, cars, books, out-

door play equipment for active play; modeling clay, clocks, boxes, containers, for creative play)

And if your child is a preschooler (aged three to five or six)

- To play with many different toys and equipment that enable preschoolers to use their imaginations? (For example, books, musical instruments, costumes)
- To choose their own activities for at least part of the day?
- To visit nearby places of interest, such as the park, the library, the fire house, a museum?

Find out about the day-care regulations in your area. In every state, all day-care centers must be licensed. According to laws that vary from state to state, family day-care homes may be licensed, certified, registered, or approved—or they may not be inspected at all.

You'll find it helpful to know about the day-care regulations in your area. For information on your state's day-care regulations, contact the licensing division in the state's health or social services department. For information on federal day-care regulations, write to the Day-Care Division, Administration for Children, Youth, and Families, Post Office Box 1182, Washington, D.C. 20013

Bibliography

Bronfenbrenner, U. (1983, May). *Family policy and family life: Friends or enemies?* Keynote address of Family Support Programs: The State of the Art. A conference sponsored by The Bush Center in Child Development and Social Policy, New Haven, Connecticut.

Bronson, M. B. (1982) *Manual for the Executive Skill Profile: A system for observing competent behaviors of preschool and primary school children.* Brookline, MA: Brookline Early Education Project.

Burkett, C. W. (1982) Effects and frequency of home visits on achievement of preschool students in a home-based early childhood education program. Journal of Educational Research, 76. 41-44.

Garber, H. L., & Heber, R. (1981) The efficacy of early intervention with family rehabilitation. In M. J. Begab, H. C. Haywood, & H. L. Garber (Eds.), *Psychosocial influences in retarded performance: Vol. II. Strategies for improving competence* (pp. 71-88). Baltimore, MD: University Park Press.

Goodson, B. D. & Hess, R. (1978). The effects of parent training programs on child performance and parent behavior. In B. Brown (Ed.), *Found: Long-term gains from early education.* Boulder, CO: Westview Press.

Gray, S. W., Ramsey, B. K., & Klaus, R. A. (1982). *From 3 to 20— The Early Training Project.* Baltimore, MD: University Park Press.

Harman, D., & Brim, O. G. (1980). *Learning to be parents: Principles, programs and methods.* Beverly Hills, CA: Sage Publications.

Hauser-Cram, P., & Pierson, D. E. (1981). *The BEEP prekindergarten curriculum: A working paper.* Brookline, MA: Brookline Early Education Project.

Howe, M. (1953). *The Negro in Ypsilanti.* Unpublished master's thesis, Eastern Michigan University, School of Education, Ypsilanti, MI.

Levin, H. M. (1977) A decade of policy developments in improving education and training for low-income populations. In R. H. Haveman (Ed.), *A decade of federal antipoverty programs: Achievements, failures, and lessons* (pp. 521-570). New York: Academic Press.

Levine, M. D., & Palfrey, J. S. (1982). The health impact of early childhood programs: Perspectives from the Brookline Early Education Project. In J. R. Travers & R. J. Light (Eds.), *Learning from experience: Evaluating early childhood demonstration programs* (pp. 57-108). Washington, D.C.: National Academy Press.

Lindner, E. W., Mattis, M. C., & Rogers, J. R. (1983). *When churches mind the children.* Ypsilanti, MI: High/Scope Press.

Ludlow, J. R., & Allen, L. (1979). The effect of early intervention and preschool stimulus on the development of the Down's syndrome child. *Journal of Mental Deficiency Research, 23, 29.*

Maisto, A. A., & German, M. L. (1979). Variables related to progress in a parent-infant training program for high risk infants. *The Journal of Pediatric Psychology, 4, 409–414.*

McCall, R. B. (1982). The process of early mental development: Implications for prediction and intervention. In N. J. Anastasiow, W. K. Frankenburg, & A. W. Fandal (Eds.), *Identifying the developmentally delayed child.* Baltimore: University Park Press.

Monroe, E., & McDonald, M. S. (1981). *Follow-up study of the 1966 Head Start program, Rome City Schools, Rome, Georgia.* Unpublished paper cited by Hubbell (1983).

Moore, M. G., Fredericks, H. D. B., & Baldwin, V. L. (1981). The long-range effects of early childhood education on a trainable mentally retarded population. *Journal of the Division for Early Childhood, 4, 93-109.*

National Association for the Education of Young Children. (1983). Progress report on the Center Accreditation Project. *Young Children, 39*(1), 35-46.

Nicol, E. H. (1979). *Enrollment and attrition: Who enrolled in BEEP and did the composition of the group change over time?* Brookline, MA: Brookline Early Education Project.

Palmer, F. H. (1983). The Harlem Study: Effects by type of training, age of training, and social class. In Consortium for Longitudinal Studies, *As the twig is bent . . . lasting effects of preschool programs* (pp. 201-236). Hillsdale, NJ: Lawrence Erlbaum Associates.

Pierson, D. E. (1973). *The Brookline program for infants and their families: The first operational year.* Brookline, MA: Brookline Early Education Project.

Pierson, D. E., Bronson, M. B., Dromey, E., Swartz, J. P. Tivnan, T., & Walker, D. K. (1983). The impact of early education. Measured by classroom observations and teacher ratings of children in kindergarten. *Evaluation Review,* 7(2), 191-216.

Ramey, C. T., & Haskins, R. (1981). The causes and treatment of school failure: Insights from the Carolina Abecedarian Project. In M. J. Begab, H. C. Haywood, & H. L. Garber (Eds.), *Psychosocial influences in retarded performance: Vol. II. Strategies for improving competence* (pp. 89-112). Baltimore, MD: University Park Press.

Simeonsson, R. J., Cooper, D. H., & Scheiner, A. P. (1982). A review and analysis of the effectiveness of early intervention programs. *Pediatrics,* 69, 635-641.

U.S. Administration for Children, Youth and Families (1983). *Ninth annual report to Congress on Head Start services.* Washington, DC: Author.

U.S. Bureau of the Census. (1982b). *Trends in child care arrangements of working mothers* (Current Population Reports: Special Studies, Series P-23, No. 117). Washington, DC: U.S. Government Printing Office.

U.S. Bureau of Education for the Handicapped. (1976). *A summary of the Handicapped Children's Early Education Program.* Washington, DC: Author.

U.S. Office of Special Education and Rehabilitative Services. (1983). *Fifth annual report to Congress on special education services.* Washington, DC: Author.

Weber, C. U., Foster, P. S., & Weikart, D. P. (1978). *An economic analysis of the Ypsilanti Perry Preschool Project: Monograph of the High/Scope Educational Research Foundation* (Number Five). Ypsilanti, MI: High/Scope Press.

White, B. L., & Watts, J. C. (1973). *Experience and environment: Major influences on the development of the young child* (Vol. 1). Englewood Cliffs, NJ: Prentice-Hall.

Yurchak, M. J. H. (1975). *Infant-toddler curriculum of the Brookline Early Education Project*. Brookline, MA: Brookline Early Education Project.

Zigler, E. F., & Trickett, D. K. (1978). IQ, social competence and evaluation of early childhood intervention programs. *American Psychologist, 33,* 789-798.

INDEX